ɁɔɁɔɔɔniiih wɔɔchɁɔɔɔnɔh

• •

Aaniiih/Gros Ventre Stories

GROS VENTRE

FIRST
NATIONS
LANGUAGE
READERS

ʔɔʔɔɔɔniiih wɔɔchʔɔɔɔnɔh

• •

Aaniiih/Gros Ventre Stories

Told by Aaniiih/Gros Ventre Elders
and/or retold by Terry Brockie

Edited and Translated by
Terry Brockie and Andrew Cowell

FIRST NATIONS
UNIVERSITY
OF CANADA

SIFC

University of Regina Press

Cover and text design: Duncan Campbell, University of Regina Press

Cover art: "Bison in Winter" by Ken Canning/iStock Photo

Illustrations in this volume are by George Shields, Jr., and were first published in *Chief Mountain's Medicine*, by members of the Gros Ventre Elders Board from the Fort Belknap Reservation, Series IV of The Indian Reading Series: Stories and Legends of the Northwest (Portland, OR: Pacific Northwest Indian Program, 1981), and in *Nee Hot & The Mouse's Eyes*, narrated by Vernie Perry and edited by Preston Stiffarm, copyright by the Fort Belknap Indian Communication, Assiniboine and Gros Ventre Indian Tribes, 1979. Used with permission of the Fort Belknap Indian Community.

Library and Archives Canada Cataloguing in Publication

Ɂɔʔɔɔɔniiih wɔɔch?ɔɔɔnɔh = Aaniiih/Gros Ventre stories / told by Aaniiih/Gros Ventre elders and/or retold by Terry Brockie ; edited and translated by Terry Brockie and Andrew Cowell.

(First Nations language readers : Gros Ventre) Aaniiih is the Gros Ventre pronunciation of Gros Ventre stories. Includes bibliographical references and index.

Issued in print and electronic formats. Text in Gros Ventre and English; translated from the Gros Ventre. Co-published by First Nations University of Canada. ISBN 978-0-88977-480-3 (softcover).—ISBN 978-0-88977-481-0 (PDF)

1. Gros Ventre language (Algonquian)—Readers. 2. Gros Ventre language (Algonquian)—Glossaries, vocabularies, etc. I. Brockie, Terry, 1969-, editor, translator II. Cowell, Andrew, 1963-, editor, translator III. First Nations University of Canada, issuing body IV. Title: Gros Ventre stories. V. Series: First Nations language readers

PM601.A56 2017   497'.33   C2017-900249-X   C2017-900250-3

10   9   8   7   6   5   4   3   2   1

University of Regina Press, University of Regina
Regina, Saskatchewan, Canada, S4S 0A2
tel: (306) 585-4758 fax: (306) 585-4699
web: www.uofrpress.ca

U OF R PRESS

We acknowledge the support of the Canada Council for the Arts for our publishing program. We acknowledge the financial support of the Government of Canada. / Nous reconnaissons l'appui financier du gouvernement du Canada. This publication was made possible through Creative Saskatchewan's Creative Industries Production Grant Program.

CONTENTS

Foreword

This latest volume of the First Nations Language Readers continues the evolution of the series and crosses further boundaries in a number of ways. Once again, we are able to present the very first collection of stories to ever see print in a particular Indigenous language of the Americas. I deliberately refer to Aaniiih/Gros Ventre in this way to highlight one obvious boundary that is being crossed. All previous volumes in this series have originated in Canada, while the people popularly known as the "Gros Ventre" are currently located solely within the United States. But such borders are recent and had no meaning for First Nations through the millennia of life here on Turtle Island, and traditional territories were not so restricted. In fact, the earliest recorded European contact with the Aaniiih took place in what is now Saskatchewan. I like to think we are helping the language to come home and be heard here once again.

And if we are to hear the language again, we need also to recognize the true name of the speakers. Thus, we also hope to redress a misnomer that has persisted among English and French speakers since that early contact when the Aaniiih or "White Clay" people were erroneously referred to as the Gros Ventre or "big bellies." Though we have retained that name here to help identify the people and language to the wider audience, we have also insisted on including a respectful and appropriate rendering of the people's own name in the hope that Aaniiih will ultimately supplant this historical error.

Along with the autonym, making the stories of the Aaniiih current is another theme of this volume. Some of the tales included herein were told by Aaniiih Elders over a century ago, though only English translations were published from that time. Others are restorations of traditional stories based on the closely related Arapaho language. I am very grateful to Terry Brockie and Andrew Cowell for their careful work in restoring these stories within the language, and honoured that they have chosen to allow this collection of Aaniiih texts to appear as the sixth volume of our series. I leave them to introduce these texts better than I possibly could.

Arok Wolvengrey
Ɂohuuciikyaaach teɁyɔɔnɔhɔɁ, 2016

Introduction:
Aaniiih/Gros Ventre Oral Narrative

We are proud to present these Aaniiih stories in their original language. This is the first collection of Aaniiih narratives ever published in the original language. (English versions of Aaniiih oral narratives can be found in Kroeber 1908a, 1908b, Curtis 1907-30, Flannery 1953, Cooper 1957, and Horse Capture 1980; Fowler 1987 provides a general history.) The language itself is part of the Algonquian family, and is most closely related to Arapaho. Aaniiih is the preferred English name – the word comes from *ʔɔʔɔɔɔniiih*, the indigenous name of the people, which is translated as "white clay."

The more commonly known name for the tribe is Gros Ventre. This is a French name and is based on a misunderstanding, according to the Aaniiih. The Aaniiih were known in the eighteenth century as the "Falls Indians" because they lived near the falls and rapids of the Saskatchewan River (which they call *ʔiwɔsiihniicaah* 'elk river'). The sign for the Falls Indians in Plains Sign Language involved both hands going out and then down in front of the body to represent the falls. This was misunderstood as "big belly" by early French arrivees, and thus the French name *gros ventre* ('big belly') was assigned to the tribe. These first contacts between whites and the Aaniiih occurred in the 1750s in the area between the north and south branches of the Saskatchewan River. The Aaniiih names for these branches are *a yah ta non*, supposedly meaning 'tall trees' (exact pronunciation and meaning uncertain, though *ʔayehi-* means 'tall') and *ʔinɔtɔnniicaah* 'belly river', respectively. (For more on Gros Ventre place names, see Cowell, Taylor and Brockie 2017.)

The Aaniiih moved south during the later eighteenth and early nineteenth centuries, onto the plains of southern Alberta and Saskatchewan and northern Montana. They eventually settled on the Fort Belknap Reservation in northern Montana, where they reside today. The reservation is bounded on the north by the Milk River (*ʔakisniicaah* 'little river') and on the south by the Little Rocky Mountains (*biiθɔtɔʔ* 'fur cap').

The stories in this collection include both "traditional" narratives and historical narratives. The former are stories which have been passed down for many centuries, as opposed to stories about events in the recent past. In English, they could be called "legends" or "myths." The latter are about events that occurred in the recent past, such as the nineteenth century. The stories come from two sources. Four of them (two war stories and two trickster stories) were taken down by Alfred Kroeber in 1901 when he visited the Fort Belknap Reservation to document Aaniiih language and culture. Using his original manuscript (National Anthropological Archives, ms 2560b), we have retranscribed and retranslated these stories. The other four trickster stories are retellings by Terry Brockie, based on Arapaho versions, and the story of Chief Mountain is likewise a retelling, based on English versions. Due to the interruption of language and culture transmission in the home, there are no longer any native speakers of Aaniiih who know and feel comfortable telling the traditional narratives in the language. There are, however, a number of younger people who are very good second-language speakers. These people (including Brockie) learned the language from the last native speakers in more or less formal study settings. There is also an immersion school. Brockie has translated four trickster stories from Arapaho (which he also has a good knowledge of) into Aaniiih, with the assistance of Andrew Cowell, who has worked extensively with the Arapaho language. The stories themselves were known earlier in Aaniiih versions, and some of them are included in Alfred Kroeber's English-language anthology of Aaniiih stories. The decision was made to translate from Arapaho to Aaniiih rather than English to Aaniiih because Arapaho and Aaniiih are closely related languages, with similar vocabulary, grammar, and word order. The Aaniiih translations follow the word order of the Arapaho as closely as possible while still maintaining the integrity of the Aaniiih language. The Arapaho stories were originally told by Richard Moss, of the Wind River Reservation in Wyoming, in 2003.

As with any language, Aaniiih has different styles of speech that are used for different purposes and different speech genres. In English we find it perfectly normal to say "thy will be done" in the Lord's Prayer, but we would never use "thy" in daily conversation. Similarly, there are certain words and grammatical features that are closely associated with traditional narratives in Aaniiih. The first of these is the narrative past tense prefix *?ou?uh-*, which is prefixed to all main verbs. This prefix has a meaning of 'it is said that...' or 'they report that...'. It indicates that the speaker does not have first-hand knowledge of the event. When this prefix is used, the verb is conjugated as if it were negative. This prefix is not used in telling everyday stories about recent events, unless the speaker wishes to emphasize that he or she is reporting hearsay.

When actions follow sequentially after the main verb, or are a consequence of the main action, we say "then," "and then," or "so then" in English. This is expressed in Aaniiih by the use of the particles (invariable words) *wɔɔkiiih* and *nahei?iiih*. When these are used, the following verb has its normal affirmative conjugation. The word *?ɔɔh* means either 'and' or 'but'. It is often used to indicate shifts in focus and continuity of narration, or to mark events which run counter to expectation, so it contrasts with *wɔɔkiiih* and *nahei?iiih*.

To quote someone's words, the verbs *wɔɔkii-* (intransitive, 's/he said') and *wɔɔkiit-* (transitive, 's/he said to him/her') are used. These are restricted to traditional narratives, and not used in ordinary conversation or everyday storytelling. They are similar in this sense to archaic English "quoth he/she" or "sayeth he/she."

A common verbal prefix used in narratives is the back-reference form *nahaa-*, meaning 'this/that aforementioned'. It is often used to sum up a discussion or description: 'and that is why...' 'so that is how...'. There is also common use of a number of particles which serve for commentary and evaluation, especially *?itɔɔwuuuh* 'truly, sure enough'.

In the modern spoken language, *nohu?* is used to indicate 'this' and *?in?* is used to indicate 'that'. In the stories from 1901, however, there are two words which mean 'this'. These are *naha?*, meaning 'this.PROXIMATE.SINGULAR', and *nohu?*, meaning 'this.OBVIATIVE' or 'this.PLURAL'. This distinction is part of the "classical" Aaniiih language, as used in these stories. "Proximate" roughly indicates the most important character in the story at the moment, while "obviative" indicates less important characters.

Finally, we should note that Aaniiih men and women speak or spoke slightly differently. Wherever women use the sounds ke, ki, or ky, men use the sounds če, či, and čy. All of the narratives that Kroeber collected were told by men, and show the men's pronunciation. Due to the interruption in language transmission in the twentieth century, this system partially broke down, and a number of native-speaker men among the last generation of speakers ended up using the women's speech form. The dictionary of Aaniiih done by Allan Taylor in 1994 reflects the women's form of the language. Brockie learned the language primarily from a woman, and also worked with a man who spoke the women's form, so his stories reflect this women's form, which has now become largely the standard form of the language, used by both men and women. There were some men who continued using the men's pronunciations, however, and a few of the younger male speakers today partially retain the male speech forms due to their work with these older men.

References

Brockie, Terry, and Andrew Cowell. 2015. "Editing a Gros Ventre (White Clay) Text." In *New Voices for Old Words: Algonquian Oral Literatures*, edited by David Costa, 9–33. Lincoln: University of Nebraska Press.

Cowell, Andrew, compiler. 2012. *Gros Ventre/White Clay Student Reference Grammar, Vol. 1.* Based on the work of Allan Taylor, with assistance from Terry Brockie and John Stiff Arm. Boulder, CO: Center for the Study of Indigenous Languages of the West.

Cowell, Andrew, Allan Taylor, and Terry Brockie. 2017. "Gros Ventre Ethnogeography and Place Names: A Diachronic Perspective." *Anthropological Linguistics.*

Cooper, John M. 1957. *The Gros Ventres of Montana: Part II. Religion and Ritual.* Edited by Regina Flannery. Washington, DC: Catholic University of America Press.

Curtis, Edward S. 1907-30. *The North American Indian.* Volume 5: 101–140; 152–54; 164–77; 180–84.

Flannery, Regina. 1953. *The Gros Ventres of Montana: Part I. Social Life.* Washington, DC: Catholic University of America Press.

Fowler, Loretta. 1987. *Shared Symbols, Contested Meanings: Gros Ventre Culture and History, 1778–1984.* Ithaca: Cornell University Press.

Horse Capture, George, ed. 1980. *The Seven Visions of Bull Lodge, as told by his daughter, Garter Snake.* Gathered by Fred P. Gone. Lincoln: University of Nebraska Press.

Kroeber, Alfred L. 1908a. *Gros Ventre Myths and Tales.* New York: American Museum of Natural History, Anthropological Papers, Vol. I, Part III: 55–139.

Kroeber, Alfred L. 1908b. *Ethnology of the Gros Ventre.* New York: American Museum of Natural History, Anthropological Papers, Vol. I, Part IV: 145–281.

Taylor, Allan. 1994. *Gros Ventre Dictionary – Prefinal Version.* 3 volumes. Fort Belknap MT: Gros Ventre Treaty Committee.

Introduction:
Aaniiih Language

Aaniiih consonants and vowels are as follows:
b, c, č (men's pronunciation), h, k, n, s, t, θ, w, y, ?
a, e, i, ɔ, o, u

The /c/ is pronounced as 'ts'. The /č/ is pronounced as 'ch' in 'church'. The /θ/ is pronounced as in 'thin'. The /ʔ/ is a glottal stop, as occurs in English "oh-oh!". The other consonants are pronounced roughly as in English, though of course not exactly so. Note that /b/ prior to /h/ sounds like English /p/. The vowels are pronounced approximately as in English set, hate, sit, hot, hope, and hut respectively. After /c/ and /s/, the vowel /i/ sounds halfway between English hit and hut. Details about pronunciation can be found in Allan Taylor's 1994 *Gros Ventre Dictionary*.

In all of the texts in this book, we use dashes to separate prefixes and suffixes from the main nouns and verbs. This is to help learners understand the structure of words, and also to make using the glossary at the end of the book easier. In this section, we briefly present the most common prefixes and suffixes (inflections) used in Aaniiih. Because there is no published grammar of Aaniiih, we give relatively extensive grammatical details here.[†] We use the women's pronunciations here.

....

† For more details, consult "Gros Ventre/White Clay Student Reference Grammar, Part One," available from the University of Colorado (http://www.colorado.edu/csilw/research/ForSale.htm).

Verbs

In this first section we cover the inflections that are added to Aaniiih intransitive verbs (technically, II and AI verbs) to indicate person and number (Table 1). These are all suffixes, added to the end of the verb.

PERSON	SINGULAR	PLURAL
0/it, they	-h	-ih/-uh
0.OBV/it, they	-nh	-niih
1/I, we (exclusive)	-nɔɔʔ	-nʔi
12/we (inclusive)	N/A	-ninʔi
2/you, you plural	-nʔɔ	-naah
3.PROX/she, he, they	-kʔi -ʔ *	-ch -ʔi *
3.OBV/she, he, they	-nicʔi	-nich
*The second forms listed for 3.PROX are used for a small set of verbs which end in a short vowel.		

Table 1. Suffixes Indicating Person and Number (for II and AI verbs)

For negative statements, questions, and other non-affirmative uses (including narrative past tense) the prefixes and suffixes are different (see Table 2 below). Prefixes (indicated by a dash at the end) are added to the beginning of the verb, while suffixes (indicated by a dash at the beginning) are added to the end of the verb. In some cases, both a prefix and a suffix are used. When a verb has no suffix, a glottal stop is simply added automatically. For 0 and 3 persons, the prefix *ʔi(i)*- can optionally be used in all cases.

PERSON	SINGULAR	PLURAL
0	-ʔ	-nɔh
0.OBV	-nʔi	-ninh
1	na-/nɔ-	na-/nɔ- VERB -bh
	neei-	neei- VERB – bh
12	N/A	ʔa-/ʔɔ- VERB -nʔi
		ʔeei- VERB -nʔi
2	ʔa-/ʔɔ-	ʔa-/ʔɔ- VERB -bh
	ʔeei-	ʔeei- VERB –bh
3.PROX	-ʔ	-nɔh
3.OBV	-nʔi	-ninh

Table 2. Prefixes and Suffixes for Negative Statements, Questions, and Other Non-Affirmatives

The prefix *chʔi-* is used to indicate negative meaning, while *ʔɔɔ-* indicates a question. The prefix *ʔooun(i)-* meaning 'should, must' also requires use of non-affirmative inflections, as does *ʔaabah-* 'possibly, maybe,' *ʔak(i)-* used to form delayed commands, and the narrative past tense *ʔouʔuh-*.

When transitive verbs occur with animate objects (technically TA verbs), a set of endings is added to the verbs, prior to the person and number markers, to indicate which person is acting on the other one. These are summarized in Table 3 below. The arrow (→) indicates "acting on."

1S / 2, I → you	-eti- / -ate-
2 / 1S, you → me	i- / -u-
1P, we→	aa-
1P, → us	-ei?aa-
1 / 2 / 3 → 3 / 3.OBV	-ɔɔ-
3 / 3.OBV → 1 / 2 / 3	-ei-

Table 3. Endings for TA Verbs

When these endings occur finally (that is, with non-affirmative verbs), the form for 3 → 3.OBV occurs as *-aa?* (3PL → 3.OBV *-aanɔh*), while the form for 3.OBV → 3 occurs as *-ah* (3.OBV → 3PL *-eiih*). These are very common endings in traditional narratives, as they occur with the narrative past tense marker *?ou?uh-*.

When a verb is transitive, but the object is inanimate (technically TI verbs), a special set of suffixes are used. These are summarized in Table 4.

	Affirmative		Non-Affirmative	
	Singular	Plural	Singular	Plural
1	-ɔwɔɔ?	-ɔwunin?i	na-/nɔ- -aa?	na-/nɔ- -aabh
1/2	N/A	-ɔwunin?i	N/A	?a-/?ɔ- -ɔwun?i
2	-ɔw?ɔ	ɔwunaah	?a-/?ɔ- -aa?	?a-/?ɔ- -aabh
3	-?ɔ	-o?	?i- -aa?	?i- -ɔwuuh
3.OBV	-ɔwunic?i	-ɔwunich	?i- -ɔwun?i	?i- -ɔwuninh

Table 4. Suffixes for TI Verbs

The endings used for commands (imperatives) are summarized in Table 5 below.

	Singular	Plural
for AI verbs	-ch	-h
for TI verbs	-ɔɔʔ	-ɔwuh
for TA verbs	**Singular Addressee**	**Plural Addressee**
1S	-ich/-uch	-ih/-uh
2	-inh/-unh	-ah
1P	-eiʔaach	-eiʔaah
2P	-inh/-unh	-ah

Table 5. Endings for Imperatives (AI, TI, and TA Verbs)

A prohibition (don't...!) is expressed using the prefix *chʔaabah-*. A future command can also be given (i.e., 'do it later') using the prefix *ʔak(i)-* (and in older sources, *ʔɔtɔn(i)-*). Note that when this is used, the verb is conjugated with non-affirmative inflections, not imperative inflections.

To indicate past tense, the prefix *nih-* is added to verbs. To indicate future tense, the prefix *ʔɔtɔn(i)-* is added. Ongoing or habitual situations are indicated using the prefix *nii- (ʔii-* non-initially), and completed situations are indicated using the prefix *ʔiis(i)-*. Other prefixes can be added with meanings of 'want to...' 'able to...' and so forth. These are listed in the glossary. These prefixes can be combined.

When a verb does not have any prefix, this indicates that the action is ongoing at the present time, or has just finished. In this case, verbs undergo a process known as "initial change." When the verb has a short vowel in the first syllable, that vowel is lengthened, so *ʔayehi-* 'tall' becomes *ʔaayeh-kʔi*, 's/he is tall'. When the verb has a long vowel in the first syllable, *-in-*

is inserted after the first consonant, so *baasɔɔ-* 'big' becomes *binaasɔɔ-h* 'it is big'.

There are also less common verbal inflections, which do nevertheless appear in the texts in this volume. This includes the iterative inflections (summarized in Table 6), which produce a meaning of 'every time...' or 'whenever...'.

PERSON	SINGULAR	PLURAL
0	-ih/-uh	-ih/-uh
0.OBV	-niih	-niih
1	-nɔɔnh	-nei?
12	N/A	-nei?
2	-nɔnh	-nei?
3.PROX	-ch, -?i	-nɔɔch, -?i
3.OBV	-nich	-nich

Table 6. Suffixes for Iterative Inflections

A second pattern are the subjunctive inflections (summarized in Table 7), which produce a meaning of 'if...' or 'when...' (in the future).

PERSON	SINGULAR	PLURAL
0, 0.OBV	-hak?ɔ/-ahk?ɔ	hakɔn?i/-ahkɔn?i
1	-nɔɔhk?ɔ	-ninahk?ɔ
12	N/A	-ninahk?ɔ
2	-nahk?ɔ	-naahak?ɔ
3.PROX, OBV	-hak?ɔ/-ahk?ɔ	-hakɔn?i/-ahkɔn?i

Table 7. Suffixes for Subjunctive Inflections

Nouns

Aaniiih nouns are either animate (NA) or inanimate (NI). The plural of nouns is either -nɔh or -iih/-uuh (ʔinenʔi 'man', ʔinennɔh 'men'). NA nouns can also be obviative (OBV), indicating lesser importance. The ending which indicates this is -nʔɔ or -iih/uuh (ʔinennʔɔ 'man (OBV)'). When something is 'in, at, on' a thing or location, the noun has a locative (LOC) suffix added. This is either -ʔa or -ʔi. When nouns are possessed, the prefixes na-/nɔ- (my), ʔa-/ʔɔ- (your), and ʔi-ʔu- (his/her) are added. When the possessor is plural, the suffix -inɔɔʔ is added, except for 1/2, where -inʔi is used.

When suffixes are added to nouns, the "full" noun stem is used, not the singular form of the noun. The difference between these two forms is complicated, and we will not go into the topic here. In the texts, where dashes are used to separate prefixes and suffixes from noun stems, we do not distinguish between singular forms of nouns and the "full" noun. So for example 'road' is byɔɔɔʔ, while the locative is byɔɔɔnʔa, which we mark as byɔɔɔn-ʔa.

A Note about the Texts that Follow

In the Aaniiih texts in this volume, where we place (?) after a word, this means that we are unsure of the exact spelling or meaning. This occurs in the texts from Kroeber. Likewise in the Kroeber texts, where we place a letter in brackets, such as [a], this indicates that the letter should be present based on our understanding of the language, but it is not recorded in Kroeber's transcription. Where brackets are used in the English translations, this indicates that the material in the brackets is not literally expressed in Aaniiih, but has been added for the sake of clarity in English.

Finally, we should note that in modern spoken Aaniiih, 1S ("I") prefixes and suffixes have been replaced by 1P (exclusive "we") prefixes and suffixes. This was a process that was already beginning to occur in 1901, and a few examples of it can be found in early documentation by the Jesuit missionary John Sifton. Taylor's 1994 dictionary reflects this change in virtually all forms. However, modern learners and speakers are now beginning to return to the classical usage, as documented here, for AI and TI verbs. This is in part because a number of the learners are familiar with Arapaho materials, which they have used to help them better understand Aaniiih, and Arapaho preserves the older forms in everyday speech. More importantly, the younger learners and speakers have access to work done by Sifton, in the early 1900s. The classical form of the language is well-documented there, and the younger speakers (a number of whom are also teachers) find that the classical forms are more "orderly" and clear for students. The degree to which the older forms are used actually varies from speaker to speaker, and the modern 1P forms are still used for 1S with TA verbs, in affirmative, non-affirmative, and imperative inflections. This is reflected in the language of Brockie's stories.

ʔɔʔɔɔniiih wɔɔchʔɔɔnɔh

Aaniiih/Gros Ventre Stories

1.

ʔɔʔɔɔɔniinennɔh
ʔɔhʔabiitɔɔθibiwɔɔch cɔɔtɔh

Stealing Horses from the Piegans

Although this story is extremely brief, we have included it here
because it is one of the very few Aaniiih texts recorded from
1901, and also because it makes a nice complement to the longer
war story also included here. The teller is unknown. It was
collected by Alfred Kroeber in Montana in 1901. The original
is in the National Anthropological Archives, manuscript 2560b,
notebook 43, p. 19 (verso). The story is told in the male language,
with /č/ replacing /k/ prior to /e/, /i/, and /y/. The Gros Ventres had
an ambivalent relationship with the Blackfeet, sometimes being
allies, other times enemies, but the group among the Blackfoot
Confederacy most often seen as enemies were the Piegans.

(1) ʔɔʔɔɔɔniinennɔh ʔɔhʔabiitɔɔθibiwɔɔch cɔɔtɔh

Ninaasou? nahaasiiih nǫǰikɔni-nɔɔ?. Nɔh ʔɔʔ-nɔɔhɔɔt-ɔwɔɔ? niiinɔn?ɔ.

Naheiʔiiih bihʔiyɔɔ-h. Naheiʔiiih ʔačinaa-nin?i.

Nɔh ?in? ?ei?iiih . . . Nɔh ʔɔʔ-itis?ɔn-ɔɔnin?i niiθou? ?iwɔsihɔɔθib-iih.

Nahaasiiih ?abiitɔɔθibiw-ɔɔnin?i cɔɔtɔh.

(1) Stealing Horses from the Piegans

The Sweet Grass Hills is where I went on the war path. And then I saw teepees.

Then it got dark. Then we approached them.

And that was when ... And then we drove off twenty horses.

That is how we stole horses from the Piegans.

2.

ʔɔʔɔɔɔniinennɔh
ʔɔhneyaacaabyiitɔɔθibyiwɔɔch
nɔɔwunɔɔčineihinɔh

The Aaniiih Try to Steal Horses from the Sioux

This narrative was told by an unknown Aaniiih man in 1901 to Alfred Kroeber. The original manuscript is in the National Anthropological Archives, manuscript 2560b. As with the other long story documented by Kroeber, he sometimes records /č/ and sometimes /ty/ for men's pronunciation. We write /č/ in all cases, but underline this where the original manuscript has /ty/. This story is told with male pronunciation. An earlier version of this story was published in 2015 (Brockie and Cowell 2015), with the transcription and translation work having been completed around 2010. The version included here should be considered more authoritative: it has several minor changes in both transcription and translation, as both authors have learned more about Aaniiih language over the intervening years. However, interested readers may want to consult the 2015 version, as it has detailed interlinear analysis and also contains the original transcription by Kroeber, in his original orthography, making it possible to evaluate our decisions in going from the original to the current version.

This story is interesting because it tells of a failure rather than a glorious success. Since stealing horses was very difficult, it is likely that many expeditions of this sort did end in failure. The story illustrates a number of moral lessons. Most importantly, it shows that one should be very careful before making boasts, and not get carried away by the moment. One can suffer great shame if unable to follow through. The man in this story who challenges the boastful singer is clearly irritated by his extravagant claims. The story also shows a loyal friend, who insists that the other men wait and look for the absent member of the party. Very likely this saved the man's life, as he might otherwise have been caught by pursuers. And finally, the story shows how natural events can cause havoc for even the best-laid plans of the experienced war leader. A sudden snowstorm followed by the coming of night leads to serious problems. This is, therefore, a classic cautionary tale, which shows the Aaniiih failing to steal horses, but succeeding nevertheless by sticking together, using their survival skills, and all returning home alive. The story also shows how the Aaniiih adopted European technologies (mirrors, telescopes) and used them in their traditional activities in innovative ways.

(2) ʔɔʔɔɔɔniinennɔh ʔɔhneyaacaabyiitɔɔθibyiwɔɔch nɔɔwunɔɔčineihinɔh

ʔouʔuh-nɔčikɔni-nɔh ʔɔʔɔɔɔniinennɔh, ʔɔɔh nɔɔǧiih-ɔɔch nɔɔwunɔɔčineihi-nɔh.

ʔei?-čaaθaanɔw-ɔɔch wɔɔǧiiih naheiʔiiih ʔɔciʔɔɔw-ɔɔch ʔɔnɔhʔɔ-hɔ? ʔah-niisi-nich ʔɔh-ʔɔʔɔɔɔci-byɔɔɔʔɔɔni-nich. ʔɔɔh ʔitɔɔwuuuh ʔouʔuh-byɔɔɔʔɔɔtɔbaa-ninh.

ʔouʔuh-naheiʔiiih ʔɔɔkɔɔci-byɔɔɔʔɔɔni-ch. ʔɔh-byɔɔɔʔɔɔtɔbaa-ch naha? ʔah-niisi-ch ʔɔnɔhʔɔ-hɔ?, "naahaasiθaa-ninʔi ʔasini-baaθeiʔɔɔ-h kɔhʔɔwuh. Taabah nɔhu? niii-ch naha? ʔeei-nɔǧiih-ɔɔɔninʔi,"† wɔɔǧii-ch naha? ʔah-niisi-ch ʔɔnɔhʔɔ-hɔ? ʔɔh-nɔci-byɔɔɔʔɔɔni-ch.

wɔɔǧiiih naheiʔiiih ʔɔɔnɔɔsibyih-eich ʔin? nɔɔčikɔniibaaa-nic? ʔin? ʔɔtn-iis-ɔɔnɔǧinɔʔɔɔ-ch.

"wɔheih," wɔɔǧiit-eich nɔhu?, "ʔɔɔtɔn-wɔtaaθaa-ninʔi. nɔhu? ʔu-yeihʔ-inɔɔ? nɔnɔɔhɔw-ɔɔneiʔi ʔininitaa?, chʔaabah-ʔaaaǧiin-ah. θɔnɔɔuh, ʔaǧeeih kɔɔθɔhaaa-bh ʔɔ-kɔciyɔɔn-inɔɔ?. ʔiniis-kɔɔθɔh-ɔwuneiʔi, nɔnɔɔhɔw-ɔɔneiʔi, chʔ-aač-ɔhkʔɔ, chʔaabah-ʔaaǧi-h; ʔati-čicikouhu-bh! ǧɔɔniiih ʔiisiiih tɔɔtounɔɔθibyaa-naahkʔɔ ʔaati-nahaakouhuuu-einaah. nɔh wʔeeitʔa ʔɔwuhuuuh byiiʔinɔɔθibyaa-naah, ʔaati-nahaatisʔɔn-ɔɔnaah ʔin? ʔɔh-čɔʔɔɔʔɔɔ-h, ʔin? ʔoh-tɔɔtɔɔnbyiicihi-ninʔi. nɔh wʔeeitʔa ʔaǧeeitʔɔ ʔihčɔʔɔɔtɔn-eininʔi, ʔaati-nahaas-tɔkohu-naah," wɔɔǧiit-eich nɔhu? nɔɔčikɔniibaaa-nic?.

wɔɔǧiiih nahaaʔiiʔ-wɔtaaθaa-ch. ʔei?-nɔɔnɔkohu-ch — ʔɔh-ʔuutaanɔw-ɔɔch nɔhu? nɔɔwunɔɔčineihi-nɔh — ʔɔɔh ʔah-niiθihi-čʔi naha? ʔɔnɔhʔɔ-hɔ? ʔouʔuh-ciicii-čɔɔtɔwuuuh. ʔini? ʔɔɔɔnʔɔ ʔohuu-chʔii-čisisiiih ʔɔčinɔʔɔɔ-ch, nii-wɔɔǧiiih niibyaaa-čʔi. ʔɔɔh ʔiniisinaaa-ch ʔitɔɔwuuuh,

---

† This is a participle meaning 'our-searched for-ones'.

(2) The Aaniiih Try to Steal Horses from the Sioux

Some Aaniiih went on a war expedition, looking for the Sioux.

When they thought they were near the Sioux, then they sent two young men on ahead to scout for them. And sure enough, they found them.

Then they came back to the others, being very careful along the way back. When the two young men who had scouted [got back], "At that place up in front of us there is a big coulee. This is where the ones we're looking for are camped," said the two young men who had scouted for the group.

So then the leader starting giving orders, as to what they all should do.

"Okay," he said to them, "when we get to the camp, if you happen to see anyone at the lodges, don't say anything to him. Right away you must strike him with your gun barrel. After you strike, if you happen to see anyone else, if he doesn't say anything, then don't say anything to him: you must run away! If you manage to capture any horses, ride them back there [where we came from]. Or if you capture a lot of them, drive them over there into the brush, where we ate our mid-day meal. Or if they catch sight of us, you must flee back there [where we came from]," the leader said to them.

So then they went to the enemy camp. When the Sioux were asleep — when they thought the Sioux were asleep — then one of the young men felt brave. Before they started to sneak up [to the camp], then he started singing [war songs]. And after he finished singing, then sure enough [he said],

"'?iininiini-noɔ?! tɔtɔh ?ih-ciitɔɔcei?ɔɔh-ɔhk?ɔ ?iwɔshɔɔθ?a niiinɔn-?a ?ɔɔt-tous-kɔsikooutis-ɔɔhɔk. ninaa-h neei-?ii?-nɔnoouθaač?i,[†] ?ohuuuh nɔčiičii-noɔ? noɔnɔnikiit?ɔ," nii-wɔɔčii-č?i naha? ?ɔnɔh?ah. Binaacininɔhouhu-ch ?ohuu-tɔɔtɔnɔɔh; kɔɔkɔn ?ou?uh-?aacinaahiiih.

woɔčiiih nahei?iiih čisisiiih ?ɔčinɔ?ɔɔ-č?i. ?ɔɔh ?iii? ?ou?uh-čɔɔɔ?.

"wɔheih," wɔɔčiit-eič?i čaaθɔɔn?ɔ naha? ?ɔɔtɔɔh ?ɔnɔh?ɔ-hɔ?, "baači?ah?iiih(?) nɔɔ-nɔɔɔci-nihii?. ?ɔɔθaa-cih wɔteeih tɔh-niiniisinei-nin?i."

"'?aastaa?!" wɔɔčii-č?i ?owɔɔh naha? ?ɔɔtɔn-kɔsikooutis-ɔɔč?i ?iwɔshɔɔθiby-iih tɔtɔh ciitɔɔcei?ɔɔn-ahkɔn?i niiinɔn-?a.

"'?aaanoouh," nii-wɔɔčiit-eič?i nohu? ?u-naacib-eeitɔn?ɔ. ?ɔtɔn-ii-niisi-nich.

"ch?iiih," nii-wɔɔčii-č?i. ?ou?uh-nahaas?i ?i-nɔneit-ɔn?ɔ.

woɔčiiih nahaas-ciinib-eič?i nohu? ?u-naacib-eeitɔn?ɔ. ?ou?uh-wɔtaakouhu-n?i. ?ɔɔh nii-wɔɔčii-naas-nahaas?i ?i-nɔneit-ɔn?ɔ.

?ɔɔh ?ou?uh-?uhčɔ?ɔɔtɔneihi-ninh ?iniitah?iiihɔh. woɔčiiih nahaas-če?iiih. tih-če?i-n?ukouhuutɔn-eič?i nohu? ?u-naacib-eeitɔn?ɔ, ?ɔɔh ?ou?uh-naaθɔɔ-nahaas?i ?i-nɔneit-ɔn?ɔ.

"?iihčɔ?ɔɔtɔn-einin?i baah," wɔɔčiit-eič?i.

---

†   This is a participle meaning 'my-reason-[for] traveling around'.

"I'm a man! Even if a horse is tied up inside a lodge, I'll cut him loose some way or another. That's why I go on war parties, to seek death," this young man was saying. But when he finished his singing, it [turned out later that it was] not true; his singing would come to nothing.

Then they started sneaking up [to the camp]. But a snowstorm came on.

"Well," one of the other young men said to [the singer], "you've really been talking a lot. Let's go into the camp, the two of us!"

"No!" said the one who was going to cut loose horses even if they were tied up inside a lodge.

"Come on!" said the one who was challenging him to join him. There will be just the two of them.

"No!" [the first one] kept saying. He was just lying on his horse.

I guess the one who was challenging him just quit talking to him. [The challenger] rode to the camp. But [the singer], he just stayed behind, lying on his horse.

And his friends were noticed [by the Sioux]. They just came right back in a hurry. When the one who had challenged him came riding back to where [the singer] was, he was still just lying on his horse.

"They spotted us friend," he said to him.

wɔɔčiiih nahaa-tɔkohu-ch. ʔouʔuh-chʔiiih . . . wɔɔčii-chʔ-
iiθɔwɔɔʔɔɔ-noh. kɔɔkɔn ʔaat-ʔiinɔči-ch ʔouʔuh-ʔuus-tɔkohu-noh.
ʔɔɔh ʔin? ʔaasi-chʔiiih naaθɔouh niihʔikouhuuh-eich, ʔouʔuh-
niitɔn-aa? ʔiniitahʔiiihih-inɔɔ? ʔah-niiθihi-nic? "ʔɔʔɔhɔɔh"
wɔɔčii-č̲ʔi, tih-tʔusib-einicʔi. ʔɔɔh ʔouʔuh-ʔuu-ʔɔɔwuhč̲ihei?
ʔɔh-č̲oʔɔoute-nh.

ʔɔh-nɔɔkɔn-ʔa wɔɔčiiih naheiʔiiih wɔɔčiiih ʔitiθič̲i-ch. ʔɔɔh
ʔɔɔtɔɔh ʔouʔuh-ʔaanisibeihiʔ; ʔouʔuh-ʔɔɔnɔɔwuhč̲ihei? čeiciθi-
ch ʔin? ʔɔh-tɔkohu-ch ʔɔh-byihʔiyɔɔ-h. ʔah-niiθihi-č̲ʔi ʔouʔuh-
chʔii-č̲eetouʔ. wɔɔčiiih nahaa-nɔɔɔt-eič̲ʔi.

"nɔɔθeei-nahʔ-eič̲ʔi, ʔɔɔtɔn-cihʔ-ɔɔtɔɔniih-ɔɔ?," wɔɔčiit-eič̲ʔi
ʔiniitahʔiiihɔh. wɔɔčiiih nahaa-č̲etɔɔʔɔɔ-nich ʔiniitahʔiiihɔh.

ʔɔh-č̲iniiθaa-nich, wɔɔčiiih naheiʔiiih č̲eʔiin-nɔči-nɔɔhɔb-
eič̲ʔi. ʔɔɔh nɔhu? ʔiič̲iθaa-nich, "ʔaanaʔaa? ʔininitaa?!"
ʔouʔuh-caaci-noʔɔouh. wɔɔčiiih naheiʔiiih ʔiiʔa-aθɔɔhɔb-eič̲ʔi
nɔč̲inɔhɔɔcɔɔɔʔ. ʔɔɔh ʔouʔuh-byiitɔbaaʔ.

"ninaani-č̲ʔi, nohʔu[č̲esi]koutɔn-[inh] ʔaθɔɔhɔbečiič̲ʔi,"
wɔɔčiit-eič̲ʔi naha? ʔaaθɔɔhɔb-eeitɔnʔɔ ʔiiʔiiih nɔč̲inɔɔhɔɔcɔɔɔʔ.
ʔɔɔh nɔɔθeeih ʔɔh-nɔɔhɔɔt-ʔɔ, ʔɔɔh nohʔuč̲esikoutɔn-eič̲ʔi,
wɔɔč̲ii-caaci-nohʔuč̲esikouhuucaaa-č̲ʔi.

"ninaani-č̲ʔi ʔitɔɔwuuuh. ʔɔtoounɔ-ɔɔtɔɔniih-ɔɔ?," wɔɔčiit-
eič̲ʔi ʔiniitahʔiii-hɔh.

ʔouʔuh-ʔiteθ-ɔɔč̲ʔi. "ʔɔ-tɔɔsɔh-ɔɔ? ʔɔ-tɔnah?" wɔɔčiit-eič̲ʔi
čaaθɔɔniiih. "Nih-nahʔ-aa?. ʔouʔuh-naač̲ikouhu-č̲ʔi," wɔɔčii-č̲ʔi.

wɔɔčiiih nah-nih-ʔiisɔ-ɔtɔniiih ʔabyiitɔɔθibyaa-ch
ʔɔʔɔɔɔniinen-noh.

So then they all took off from there. They didn't . . . they couldn't see where they were going [due to the snow]. They ended up scattered all over after they fled. And while they were still riding hard, they heard one of their friends say "Ouch!" when he was thrown from his horse. [The horse] was going down the slope of a bank.

When morning came, then they all stumbled around until they found each other. Some of them had been injured; the horses ran down [coulees] and [the riders] didn't know where they were going as they fled in the dark. One of them was missing; they had left him behind.

"Maybe [the Sioux] killed him, we can't wait for him," his friends said [to his best friend]. So then his friends set off from there.

Once they had gone a long ways, then they looked back to try and see him. And from back where they had come from, "There's someone!" [one of them said]. He was coming towards them. So then one of them looked at him through a telescope. He was on foot.

"That one, signal him with a mirror," the one looking at him with the telescope said to the others. And when he saw they were shining the mirror at him as a signal, then he signaled back with a mirror.

"That's him, for sure. We must wait for him," [his best friend] said to his other friends.

Once he had reached them, "What did you do with your horse?" one of them asked him.

"I killed it. It was exhausted from running hard," he said.

So that was how the Aaniiih failed to steal horses.

3.

nih?ɔɔtɔh ?ɔh?ɔkɔɔciiniiničʔi

Trickster Gets a New Wife

This is a portion of a longer story which is included in Alfred Kroeber's English-language anthology of Gros Ventre stories (1908a:70). The teller is unknown. Kroeber collected the story in Montana in 1901. The original is in the National Anthropological Archives, manuscript 2560b, notebook 43, p. 7. Like all the material Kroeber collected, this story is told in the male language, with /č/ replacing /k/ prior to /i/, /e/, and /y/. In the full version of the story, Nih?ɔɔtɔh is happy to have his new wife, and travels on. He finds another man crying for his own wife, and Nih?ɔɔtɔh doubles his wife into two and gives one to that man. He does this three times successfully, but when he tries to do it a fourth time, his wife falls dead.

15

(3) nih?ɔɔtɔh ?ɔh?ɔkɔɔciiniinič?i

Nih?ɔɔtɔh ?iniin?ɔ ?ou?uh-nɔɔnɔnehi-n?i. ?ɔɔh ?ou?uh-biiwouhu? čyɔ?ɔtinin-?i.

?ɔɔh ?inen-n?ɔ ?ou?uh-?itiθ-a?. Nɔh wɔɔčiit-eič?i,

"Yah, nih?ɔɔtɔh, ?eei-thuuci-biiwɔɔh?" wɔɔčiit-eič?i.

"?ayɔ?ɔɔ?, nɔh natiθaha? nɔɔnɔneh-č?i," wɔɔčiit-ɔɔč?i.

Nɔh nohu? ?inen-n?ɔ wɔɔčiit-ɔɔnic?[†] ?iniin?ɔ,

"Wɔheih bitabyih, ?atib-ɔ?ɔɔci-too?uθaa-ch!"

Naaθ?a ?ou?uh-nɔwuh-aan?i,[‡] nɔh nohu? yinaanɔ?ɔwɔɔ-h, ?ou?uh-nahei?-tɔ?ɔw-ɔɔnic?. ?ɔɔh ?ou?uh-niyaaθesikouhu-ninh ?iθaa-nɔh.

"Wɔhei nih?ɔɔtɔh, nohu? čaaθ?ɔɔ[n]?ɔ, ?itin-inh! ?ɔtɔn-niiw-ɔɔ?," wɔɔčiit-eič?i.

....

† This inflection indicates one obviative acting on another, as opposed to more usual -ɔɔč?i.

‡ This inflection indicates one obviative acting on another, as opposed to more usual -aa?.

16

(3) Trickster Gets a New Wife

Nih?ɔɔtɔh's wife died, and he was crying on a hill.

And a man came to him. And [the man] said to him,

"Hey, Nih?ɔɔtɔh, why are you crying?" [the man] said to him.

"Well, my wife has died," [Trickster] said to him.

And this man told his [own] wife,

"Well old woman, walk over there facing away from me and stop!"

Three times he made a motion to smack her, and on the fourth time, then he hit her. And [then] there were two women where she was standing.

"Well Nih?ɔɔtɔh, this other one, take her! You will have her as a wife," [the man] said to [Nih?ɔɔtɔh].

4.

Nih?ɔɔtɔh nɔh ?ɔɔciihihɔ?

Trickster and the Mice's Sun Dance

This story was collected by Alfred Kroeber. He notes that it was told to him by Paul Plumage, on Sunday, February 17, 1901. The original text is in the National Anthropological Archives, manuscript 2560b, Notebook 41, pp. 57-64. An English translation of this specific version of this text is in Kroeber 1908a: 68-69. It is told in men's language. The modern Aaniiih dictionary is in women's language. Wherever ke-, ki- and ky- occur in the modern language, the men's language uses če-, či-, and čy-. Note that Kroeber wrote this sound as č on some occasions and ty on others. For the sake of consistency and learners, we write č on all occasions, but for the sake of documentation, we underline the sound (č) when it is written ty in the original manuscript.

There are a number of *nih?ɔɔtɔh* (trickster) stories that make up part of a cycle related to the Sun Dance, for both the Aaniiih and Arapaho peoples. This story is part of that cycle. It contains two parts of the cycle. The first part is the trickster's discovery of the mice having a Sun Dance in an elk skull, and getting his head stuck in the skull when he becomes too curious about what is going on inside there. Secondly, since he cannot see, he falls into a stream, floats downstream, is found by some young women, and is attracted to the women. He gets them to hit him on the head and break open the skull so that he can escape.

There are traditionally four plants that he encounters as he wanders blindly towards the stream, each one ecologically more closely associated with running water. In this version, only three of the plants are named: the chokecherry, cottonwood, and willow, with the stream serving as the fourth encounter. In other versions of the encounter with the young women, they offer to delouse the trickster and he falls asleep in their laps. They then fill his hair with burrs, and he is forced to shave his head since he can't get the burrs out. When he returns home to his wife, she asks "Why are you in mourning, who died?" since he has cut his hair. He says "I heard you died," and his wife says, "What a fool my husband is."

(4) Nih?ɔɔtɔh nɔh ?ɔɔciihihɔ?

Nih?ɔɔtɔh ?ou?uh-cetɔ?ɔɔ?. ?ɔɔɔn?ɔ ?aasiθaa-ǧ?i, ?ou?uh-niitɔwɔɔt-?ɔ ?ɔθeeihɔɔwuh ?ɔh-čyaa?aanɔɔni-h. ?ou?uh-nahei?-tou?uθaa-ǧ?i. ?ɔɔh [?ou?uh]th?-eei?in? tɔɔnh ?ɔh-čyaa?aanɔɔni-h ?ɔθeeihɔɔwuh. ?ɔɔh ?ou?uh-ch?eei?in? tɔɔnh ?ɔh-naani?.

?ɔɔh ?in? ?ɔh-niicii-ǧ?i, ?ou?uh-?eeinɔɔtaa? ?iwɔsiihɔɔchɔ?ɔɔ?. ?ou?uh-nahei?-čyaanɔci?. ?ɔɔh ?in? ?ɔh-čyaanɔci-č?i, ?ou?uh-nahei?-[n]ɔɔɔθaanɔɔni-h nɔh(?) ?in? ?ɔθeeihɔɔwuh.

"Yah, ?iič?i ?ɔt-ooun-naa?!"

?ɔɔh niibineeihiih nɔtinɔɔh-ɔwuh. wɔɔčiiih nahei?iiih ?iiwɔɔci?ɔɔ-ǧ?i. ?ɔɔh ?ou?uh-nɔɔθɔɔ-?ɔθeeihiinɔhwɔɔ-nin?ɔ ?ɔɔciihihɔ?.

Nɔh ?un? ?aasi-iiwɔɔci?ɔɔ-č?i, baas-tɔnɔɔ?ɔɔ-ch! nii-wɔɔǧii-č?i ?in? ?ɔh-tɔnɔǧi-n?i.

?in? nih-?iič-iiwɔɔci?[oo]-č?i, ?ɔɔh ?ou?uh-baas-tɔnɔɔ?ɔɔ-n?i. ?in? ?aatɔsi-nihiit-o?, ?ei?iiih, ?ou?uh-baasiiih tɔnɔɔ?ɔɔ?. ?ɔɔh ?in? ?ei?-iisiiih behi-ciita?aanɔɔ?ɔɔ-h, ?in? ?ɔɔciihihɔ? ?ou?uh-neih?aakouhu-ninh.

?ou?uh-naanihi?-ciiciikɔyaaa?. ?ou?uh-nahaas-nei?inɔɔ?ɔɔ? ?in? ?ɔɔchɔ?ɔɔn-?a.

Wɔɔǧiiih na?-nih-?ii?-biiwouhu-ǧ?i, ?ohuu-niiǧɔuhun?(?) niisi-n?iǧii-ǧ?i. Tɔtɔh ?ou?uh-?uu-wɔɔčii-ch?ii-nɔɔhɔɔcaaa?

Wɔɔǧiiih nahei?iiih kɔheei-ǧ?i, ?ɔɔh ?in? ?ihči?teit-?ɔ.

"?ɔ-thuutehi??" nii-wɔɔčiit-ɔɔč?i.

(4) Trickster and the Mice's Sun Dance

Nih?ɔɔtɔh set off. When he had not yet reached his destination, he heard the noise of a Sun Dance. Then he stopped. He wanted to know where the noise of the Sun Dance was coming from. He did not know what the noise was.

And at the place where he was standing, there was an elk skull laying there. Then he sat down. And at the place where he sat down, then there was a lot of noise, of that Sun Dance.

"Well! This must be the place!"

And he was secretly trying to see it. And then he peeked in through a hole. And the mice were still holding a Sun Dance there.

And as he was looking through the hole, "You be larger!" he said to the hole [wider?].

That place where he was peeking in got larger. Every time he said that, afterwards, then it got bigger. As soon as he got his head all the way in there, the mice fled in every direction.

And then he was really swearing up a storm. And that's how his head got stuck inside that skull.

I guess then he began to cry because he did not know how to make it right again. I guess he couldn't even see anything.

Then he stood up. And that's when he hit something hard with his foot.

"Who are you?" he said.

"Ninaa-nɔɔʔ ʔɔnɔɔɔwouʔu-nɔɔʔ."

"ʔihʔɔɔʔ naa-nɔɔhɔkʔa čγaasɔʔ-ɔwɔɔʔ niicaah."

Nɔh caaaʔ ʔihči?teit-ʔɔ ʔitɔʔɔɔt(ʔ). nih-biisicaaaʔ.

"ʔɔ-thuutehiʔʔ" wɔɔčii-č̣ʔi.

"ʔɔɔhɔɔči-nɔɔʔ" wɔɔčiit-eičʔi

"ʔihʔɔɔʔ" naa-nɔɔhɔkʔa kʔiiih ʔaacineeih čγaasɔʔ-ɔwɔɔʔ ʔinʔ
niicaah.

Nɔh caaaʔ naheiʔ-[n]aac-četɔʔɔɔʔ. ʔɔɔh caaaʔ ʔihči?teit?ɔ
ʔitɔʔɔɔt(ʔ).

"ʔɔ-thuutehiʔʔ" wɔɔčii-č̣ʔi.

"Neniicɔɔsi-nɔɔʔ," wɔɔč̣iit-eičʔi.

"ʔihʔɔɔ," wɔɔčii-č̣ʔi. "naa-nɔɔhɔkʔa ʔaacineeih čγaasɔʔ-
ɔwɔɔʔ ʔinʔ niicaah."

Wɔɔčiiih naheiʔiiih nistoo-čibiθaaʔ. ʔɔɔh ʔaasiiih nistoo-
čibiθaa-[č]ʔi, ʔouʔuh-ʔɔɔwooubeihiʔ.

"ʔɔ-thuutehiʔʔ" wɔɔčii-č̣ʔi.

ʔouʔuh-tibyaaʔaanaasʔ.

Wɔɔčiiih naheiʔiiih ʔɔɔwuniihoouʔɔɔ-čʔi. ʔɔɔh ʔaatoouʔɔɔ-
čʔi, ʔiitaaʔ ʔouʔuh-ʔɔɔtaaʔ. ʔɔɔh ʔouʔuh-touθibyiitɔɔnʔ.
ʔinʔ touθibyiihyɔh ʔaas-nɔɔhɔb-eič̣ʔi, "wɔɔtɔh! Naanaʔaaʔ
cinaatoouʔɔɔ-č̣ʔi bɔhʔɔɔɔʔ!"

ʔɔɔh ʔouʔuh-bhʔi-noouh tɔkohu-ninʔɔ. ʔinʔ ʔɔh-nah-niiʔ-
nɔʔoouʔɔɔ-čʔi, wɔɔčii-čʔi "nii-baaθih-ouh, nɔɔtooubih-einɔɔʔ(ʔ)
ʔakisiiθaa-n."

ʔinʔ ʔaasiiih ʔiisi-nihii-čʔi, ʔah-niisi-nich ʔakisiiθaa-nɔh
ʔouʔuh-nii[θ]ʔ-seiʔihčehi-ninʔɔ. ʔɔɔh nohuʔ naheiʔiiih ʔiitɔniiih
ʔiciinitaan-eičʔi. Naheiʔiiih nɔʔoouθih-eič̣ʔi.

22

"I am Chokecherry."

"Okay, I must be pretty close to the river."

And again he hit something with his foot. He felt something.

"What are you?" he said.

"I am Cottonwood," it said to him.

"Okay, I must be very close to the river again."

And then he set off again. And again he felt something with his feet.

"Who are you?" he said.

"I am Willow," it said to him.

"Okay," he said. "I must be very close to a river."

Then he walked carefully. And as he was carefully walking along, he suddenly felt himself going down.

"Who are you?" he said.

Then there was the sound of a splash.

Then he floated down [the river]. The place where he floated, there was a camp of lodges. There was a swimming party there then. As soon as those swimmers saw him, "Look out! The water monster is floating towards us!"

Then all of them fled to the bank. When he was floating close to them, he said, "I only want young women to come to me."

As soon as he said it, two of the young women jumped into the water. They went on each side and caught his horns. And then they pulled him to the shore.

nɔh ʔah-niiθehi-nicʔ, ʔiis-nʔuθaa-[č]ʔi, ʔɔɔh ʔinʔ ʔah-niiθehi-nicʔ ʔouʔuh-toun-aaʔ. Nah-niičɔɔw-ɔɔčʔi.

ʔinʔ ʔɔɔtoowuuh, ʔaas-nɔɔhɔb-eičʔi ʔouʔuh-ʔickuut-ɔɔčʔi, c̲aaθɔɔnɔh ʔinʔ ʔačisiiθaa-nɔh, ʔouʔuh-behiiih ʔɔɔsiiih č̲ʔaacikouhu-ninh.

"Nihʔɔɔtɔh caaayɔʔɔɔtaa-č̲ʔi," wɔɔčii-bahʔi-nihii-nich.

ʔinʔ ʔačisiiθaa-nʔɔ, ʔih-ʔickuut-ɔɔnʔɔ,† ʔiinɔɔnʔɔ wɔɔčii-nihʔikouhu-nicʔ nɔhciiih toθooʔ. ʔɔɔh ʔouʔuh-naaθoouh niičaab-aaʔ. Wɔɔčiiih naheiʔiiih tʔɔɔt-ɔwunich tɔnisɔʔɔɔ-n nohuʔ ʔuθaa-nʔɔ.

wɔɔčii-č̲ʔi nihʔɔɔtɔh, "ʔɔɔtɔɔhɔɔʔ wouʔu-nɔɔʔ ʔɔ-tɔɔnah. nah-niiʔ-čyɔʔɔh-einɔɔʔ tɔɔtɔɔniinit-ʔa," wɔɔč̲iit-ɔɔč̲ʔi.

ʔinʔ ʔiθaa-nʔ wɔɔčiiih naheiʔiiih tʔɔɔt-ɔwunich tɔɔtɔɔnii[ni] t-ʔa. ʔɔɔh ʔouʔuh-nihʔaatɔɔʔɔh-ɔwunʔi ʔinʔ ʔɔɔchɔʔɔɔn-ʔɔ.

wɔɔč̲iiih naheiʔ-kɔheeisihǧehi-č̲ʔi, ʔouʔuh-tɔkohuʔ. ʔouʔuh-behi-nihʔɔɔɔn-aʔ. Nahaʔ behi-cɔɔni-itibeh-čʔi.

Naaheiʔis-ʔa.

---

† This is a participle meaning 'his-grabbed-one', 'the one he grabbed'.

And one of them, after he got there, and he caught one of them. He laid with her.

And the rest, as soon as they saw him grabbing her, the other young women, they all ran back towards home.

"Trickster is taking her virginity," they were all saying.

That young woman, the one whom he had caught, well her mother came running with a mortar. He was still there laying there with her. Then this woman hit him in the butt.

Trickster said, "The hammer is helping me out with your daughter. The place where you can kill me is right between the horns," he said to her.

That woman hit him right in the middle of the head. And she shattered that skull to pieces with the hammer.

Then he jumped up, and ran away. Everyone was chasing after him. This trickster could not be caught by anyone.

That's as far as it goes.

5.

Nih?ɔɔtɔh
?ɔh?oouckuukiik?i ?isiiθeeih

Trickster Throws His Eyes

BY TERRY BROCKIE, BASED ON AN ARAPAHO ORIGINAL,
WITH ASSISTANCE FROM ANDREW COWELL

This is another classic trickster story, known by both the Aaniiih and the Arapaho. Another version of this story is included in English in Kroeber 1908a: 70. Although this version does not say so explicitly, part of the attraction of the ability to throw one's eyes is that the eyes perch on top of a tree, and one can see buffalo far off in the distance. This power could thus be useful for hunting and feeding the people. But according to many Aaniiih stories such power should only be used in times of necessity. The trickster, on the other hand, wastes the power simply to amuse himself. In some versions of the story, the chickadee actually gives his eyes to the trickster, and that is why "the trickster has small, beady eyes." This story is also commonly told in Aaniiih using the mouse instead of the bird in this text. It explains why the mouse has his eyes on the top of his skull: this was due to Nih?ɔɔtɔh placing them in the wrong place after borrowing the mouse's eyes to retrieve his in the tree.

(5) Nih?ɔɔtɔh ?ɔh?oouckuukiik?i ?isiiθeeih

Nih?ɔɔtɔh ?ou?uh-?ɔɔwuniihiθaa?. ?ou?uh-?iteθ-aa? nii?ihyɔhɔ?. Nohu? nii?ihyɔhɔ? ?ou?uh-?oouckuukii-n?i ?isiiθeeih. "Tɔɔtɔɔkɔɔtɔɔh," nih-?eihi-nic?i. ?ou?uh-k?i-teeinɔwɔɔ-ninh ?isiiθeeih.

"Wuuuh," ?eih-k?i nihɔɔ?tɔh. "Bitaanih-ei?aach," naha? wɔɔkii-k?i.

"Nahaasiiih," wɔɔkiit-eik?i nohu? nii?ihyɔhɔ?.

?ɔɔh ?ou?uh-nih?inaa?.

"Wɔheih," wɔɔkiit-eik?i."Kooun yaan?a ?ak-niiskyɔɔ?," wɔɔkiit-eik?i

?ou?uh-ketɔɔ?ɔɔ?. Naha? nih?ɔɔtɔh nah-nih-?iiskyɔɔ-k?i. ?ɔɔh yɔɔtɔn?a ?ou?uh-nahaaskyɔɔ-k?i. Kɔsiitiniih ?ou?uh-baackyɔɔ?.

Kouciiih ?ou?uh-c?ɔci?. ?ɔɔh ?isiiθeeih ?ou?uh-?oouta-ninh. "Tɔɔtɔɔkɔɔtɔɔh," ?eih-k?i. ?ɔɔh ?oh?uh-ch?ii-k?i-teeinɔɔ?ɔɔ-ninh ?isiiθeeih.

Nohu? nii?ihyɔhɔ? ?ou?uh-?iteθ-a?.

"Kooun?ɔ yaan?a ?ak-niiskyɔɔ?, nih-?iit-aan?o," wɔɔkiit-eik?i.

Nahei?iiih k?i-teeinɔwuun-eik?i. ?ɔɔh ?ou?uh-naani? biikiyeeih.

Nahaasiiih.

(5) Trickster Throws His Eyes

Nih?ɔɔtɔh was walking downstream. He came upon a little bird. This bird tossed up his eyes so that they hung on top of a tree. He would say "tɔɔtɔɔkɔɔtɔɔh." Then his eyes would come back in their sockets.

"Hey!!!" Nih?ɔɔtɔh said. "Give me this power," he said to the bird.

"Leave it alone," the little bird said to him.

But [Nih?ɔɔtɔh] insisted.

"All right then," the little bird said to him. "But just four times you must do it," it said to him.

Nih?ɔɔtɔh set off. This Nih?ɔɔtɔh, he did just like the bird had done. But he did it five times. Then suddenly he was finished.

He sat there for a long time. His eyes were still hanging up there. He would say, "tɔɔtɔɔkɔɔtɔɔh." But his eyes would not come back in the sockets.

Then the little bird came upon the Trickster.

"Just four times you must do it, I told you," he said to him.

Then he made the eyes go back in the sockets for him. And that was the chickadee.

That's how the story goes.

6.

Nih?ɔɔtɔh nɔh cʔiisikɔhɔʔ

Trickster and the Ducks

BY TERRY BROCKIE, BASED ON AN ARAPAHO ORIGINAL,
WITH ASSISTANCE FROM ANDREW COWELL

This is a story which is widely known among the Aaniiih as well as the Arapaho. A different version is included in English in Kroeber 1908a: 71. It provides a classic lesson about excess gullibility and excess obedience, as well as the way that one person willing to break the rules can save everyone. Quite often, this person is portrayed as staying "in back" or "off to the side" rather than coming forward to the front. There are longer versions of the story, in which the Trickster tries to cook and eat the ducks he has killed but is robbed of his gains by Coyote.

(6) Nih?ɔɔtɔh nɔh c?iisikɔhɔ?

Nohu? Nih?ɔɔtɔh ?ou?uh-bitɔɔɔh-aa? nohu? c?iisikɔ-hɔ?. "Wɔheih," wɔɔkiit-ɔɔk?i nohu? c?iisikɔ-hɔ? "?ɔɔtɔn-bitɔɔɔh-aanaah. Nahei?iiih ?ɔɔtɔn-no?uuθɔ?ɔɔ-naah. ?ɔɔtɔn-bitɔɔɔh-aanaah. Tɔɔnh nii-kɔɔnɔɔku-k?i ?ɔɔtɔn-ii-neki-k?i," wɔɔkiit-ɔɔk?i.

Nahei?iiih, kyessi-niibyaaa-k?i. Niniibyɔɔɔn-ɔɔk?i.

"hɔei?ei hɔei?ei hɔyeiyei ?ɔɔ?ei?ei."

"Tɔɔnh nii-kɔɔnɔɔku-k?i ?ɔɔtɔn-ii-neki-k?i."

?ohuu-kewɔhwɔɔ-nɔɔch, ?ou?uh-?ickuut-aa?. ?ou?uh-teb?aakuut-aa?. kyaaθɔɔn?ɔ ?ou?uh-kewɔhwɔɔ? ?ou?uh-?ickuut-aa?, teb?aakuut-aa?. nahei?iiih kyaabi-t?usit-?ɔ.

?ɔh-niiθeh-k?i ?ou?uh-?iit?a, nɔkɔteeih ?ou?uh-bitaaa?. ?ou?uh-kɔɔkɔɔnɔɔcɔ?ɔɔ-k?i. Nahei?iiih nɔɔhɔw-ɔɔk?i niistɔɔ-nic? nohu? Nih?ɔɔtɔh.

"?ɔ?eeih tɔkɔhu-h! ?ɔɔtɔn-nɔɔ?ɔɔh-einin?i."

Nahei?iiih beihi-kesisɔh?uh-ch.

Noh nahaasiiih. Nahei?iiih nih-?iise-ei?inɔn-eik?i nih-?iis-ciinaanikyoo-k?i nohu? Nih?ɔɔtɔh. Nih-?ii-b?i-teb?aakuut-ɔɔk?i.

Noh naahaaθɔɔ-h nohu? wɔɔcɔh?ɔɔɔ?.

(6) Trickster and the Ducks

This Trickster made these ducks dance. "Woheih," he said to these ducks, "I am going to make you dance. And then you will close your eyes. I am going to make you dance. Whoever opens their eyes, he will die," he said to them.

And then he started to sing. He is singing for them.

Song: First line no meaning.

Song: Second line: "Whoever opens his eyes will die."

Each time one of them danced past him, he grabbed him. He broke his neck/knocked off his head. Another one danced past, and he grabbed him and cut his head off. And then he just tossed the head off to the side.

But one of them over there, I guess, was dancing off to the side. He slowly opened his eyes. And then he saw what this Trickster was doing.

"Hey, flee! He will slaughter us!"

And then they all started to fly away.

And that's how the story goes. And that is how this one knew how this Trickster was up to no good. He was just cutting their heads off.

And that's how this story goes.

7.

Nih?ɔɔtɔh nɔh kɔɔ?ɔhwuh

Trickster and the Coyote

**BY TERRY BROCKIE, BASED ON AN ARAPAHO ORIGINAL,
WITH ASSISTANCE FROM ANDREW COWELL**

This is one of many stories found in both Aaniiih and Arapaho where the Trickster gets into competition with Coyote. Trickster is always overconfident, always looking to show off, and Coyote always wins. This story also shows the familiar Aaniiih pattern of four stages in a story, since four is the most sacred number traditionally in Aaniiih culture. The story also illustrates Trickster's tendency to get distracted by romance when he should be thinking about other things.

(7) Nih?ɔɔtɔh nɔh kɔɔ?ɔhwuh

Nohu? Nih?ɔɔtɔh ?ou?uh-?iteθ-aa? ?in? kɔɔ?ɔwuhɔ?. ?ou?uh-?iteθ-aa?.

"?aacineei-nɔɔɔtehi-nɔɔ?," wookiit-ook?i nohu? kɔɔ?ɔwuhɔ?. ?ɔɔtɔni-iiθɔɔhɔɔch-aan?ɔ na-kiiθe?iib?i."

"?aaa?, wɔheih caac-?iiθɔɔhɔɔch-ei?aach!"

"wɔheih ?iik?a ?ak-naac-tɔyɔɔhɔb-ei?aa?. ?ɔɔtɔnɔ-ɔɔctaateikouhu-nɔɔ?. Byɔɔkouciiih ?ak-caacɔ-ɔɔwuθaa?.

Nahei?iiih naac-?ɔɔctaateiθaa-k?i nohu? kɔɔ?ɔhwuh. Nahei?iiih nɔɔhɔw-ɔɔk?i nɔɔsikyɔhɔ? ?ou?uh-?eeinɔci-n?i.

"?aaa?." ?ou?uh-nɔɔnɔɔ?aaθɔɔtɔn-aa?. ?ou?uh-baa-benɔɔb-aa?. "?aaa?, ch?iiih ninaan-n?ɔ Nih?ɔɔtɔh." ?ou?uh-naani-n?i.

Nahei?iiih kei?-kɔheei-k?i nohu? Nih?ɔɔtɔh. "Wɔheih kyaaθey?ɔ ?ɔɔtɔniiih..."

tɔɔθ?ɔ ?ou?uh-caac-?ɔɔctaateiθaa? nohu? kɔɔ?ɔhwuh. ?ou?uh-nɔɔhɔb-aa? bih?ihii? ?ou?uh-θei?isine-n?i.

"?aaa?" ?ou?uh-nɔɔnɔɔ?aaθɔɔtɔn-aa?. "?aaa?, ch?iiih. ninaani-n?ɔ Nih?ɔɔtɔh."

wɔheih nahei?iiih tɔɔθ?ɔ k?i-kɔheei-k?i nohu? Nih?ɔɔtɔh. ?ou?uh-caac-?ɔɔctaateikouhu?. ?iikii? ?ou?uh-k?i-t?usibikik?i. Wɔɔw?u ?iwɔsiihii?, ?ou?uh-naani-n?i θei?isine-n?i. ?ɔ?uh-?aacinaa-kɔskeeihi-n?i.

Tɔɔθ?ɔ nahei?-caac-k?in?uθaa-k?i nohu? kɔɔ?ɔhwuh. "?ɔ?eeih," nɔɔθɔθɔɔhɔw-ɔɔk?i nih-?aacinaa-kɔskeeihi-nic? ?in?. "?aaa?," ?ou?uh-nɔɔ?aa-baabenɔɔb-aa?. "?aaa?, ch?iiih ninaani-n?ɔ Nih?ɔɔtɔh ch?iiih."

Nahei?-k?i-kɔheei-k?i nohu? Nih?ɔɔtɔh. "ch?iiih, ch?iiih."

(7) Trickster and Coyote

This Nih?ɔɔtɔh happened to meet that coyote. He happened to meet him.

"I am the most powerful," he said to this coyote. "I will show you my power."

"Yes, okay then show me!"

"Well, here you must wait for me a little while. I will run on down the stream. Later, you must come on down to where I'll be, after a while," [Nih?ɔɔtɔh said to Coyote].

Then [after waiting a while], Coyote set off from there downstream. Then he saw an antelope lying there.

"Hmm," he walked all around it. He sniffed all around it. "Hmm, no, it's you, Nih?ɔɔtɔh." It was him.

Then Nih?ɔɔtɔh got back up. "Well I'm going to try again."

Once again this coyote came down on the stream [after him]. That's when he saw a deer lying there.

"Hmm," he walked all around it. "Hmm, no, it's you, Nih?ɔɔtɔh."

Well, then once again Nih?ɔɔtɔh got back up. [Níh?ɔɔtɔh] ran on down along the stream some more. Right there he plopped himself down again. Now an elk, that was what it was lying there. It was really plump.

Once again this coyote arrived there. "Oooh," he looked eagerly at that really plump that one. "Hmm," he sniffed all around it. "Hmmm, no, it's you, Nih?ɔɔtɔh, no."

Then Nih?ɔɔtɔh got up again. "No, no," [Coyote said to him].

Wɔheih kyaaθeyʔɔ yinaanɔʔɔwɔɔʔ. Wɔɔwʔu naheiʔ-naac-
ʔɔɔctaateiθaa-kʔi nohuʔ Nihʔɔɔtɔh. Wɔɔwʔu ʔanaakyaanʔɔ
ʔouʔuh-θeiʔisine-nʔi ʔatibiiih. kʔi-tɔɔθʔɔ ʔouʔuh-kɔskeeihi-nʔi.
ʔouʔuh-wɔɔtaaʔ ʔɔθaanɔh.

ʔouʔuh-nʔuθaaʔ. ʔouʔuh-nɔɔnɔɔʔaaθɔɔtɔn-aaʔ nohuʔ
kɔɔʔɔhwuh. "ʔaaaʔ, chʔiiih ninaani-nʔɔ Nihʔɔɔtɔh."

"Wɔheih biikʔa. ʔɔɔtɔni-iiθɔɔhɔɔch-aanʔɔ na-kiiʔθeʔiibʔi.
ʔiikʔi ʔak-caac-tɔyɔɔhɔwʔu."

Byɔɔkouciiih ʔak-caac-ʔɔɔctaateiθaaʔ. "ʔɔɔtɔn-naac-
ʔɔɔctaateikouhu-nɔɔʔ." byɔɔkouciiih naheiʔ-caac-ketʔɔɔʔɔɔ-kʔi
nohuʔ Nihʔɔɔtɔh. ʔiikʔi caacaabiiih byɔɔɔn-ʔa ʔɔhʔɔnaakyaan-
ʔa ʔouʔuh-niitɔn-aaʔ ʔiθaa-nʔɔ ʔouʔuh-ʔuu-biiwouhu-nʔi.
byɔɔkouciiih ʔouʔuh-nɔɔhɔb-aaʔ naheiʔiiih naaciih-ɔɔkʔi.

"Wɔheihʔ ʔaayouʔ ʔaayouʔ ʔaayouʔ ʔɔhuu-biiwouhu-nʔɔʔ?"

"Niiθenɔɔʔ nɔh neinɔɔʔ nih-nɔɔɔhisʔɔn-eiʔaach. Neei-
chʔiiyeeihiʔ. Neei-chʔeeiʔin-ooʔ tɔɔnh ʔɔɔtɔn-kewʔɔɔ-nɔɔʔ."

"ʔaaaʔ, ʔɔɔtɔn-nitɔɔ-nɔɔʔ," wookiit-ɔɔkʔi nohuʔ Nihʔɔɔtɔh.
"ɔɔtɔn-nʔi-ʔaatiniih-aaanʔɔ. ʔɔɔtɔn-nʔi-niis-nitɔɔ-ninʔɔ. Nii-
nʔi-ʔiiinɔɔʔaa-nɔɔʔ ʔaanaasiiih. ʔɔɔtɔniiih ʔɔɔtɔni-chʔii-
nɔɔnɔɔʔouhuʔ. ʔɔɔtɔni-chʔii-nɔɔnɔɔʔouhuʔ. ʔɔɔtɔn-bhʔi-
niiniistɔn-aanʔɔ. ʔɔɔtɔniiih . . . ʔɔɔtɔn-ii-niiθʔu-niis-nitɔɔ-ninʔɔ.
ʔɔɔtɔn-naacθɔt-aanʔɔ," wɔɔkiit-ɔɔkʔi nohuʔ Nihʔɔɔtɔh.

"Nahaah," wookiit-eikʔi nohuʔ ʔiθeihyɔhɔʔ, "ʔɔɔtɔn-niʔiiih,
nahaah."

"Wɔheih ʔɔɔtɔn-nɔɔnɔθɔniθaa-ninʔɔ ʔɔɔh niitɔwuuuh niitɔh
ʔɔɔtɔn-niitɔniki-ninʔɔ. ʔɔɔtɔniiih naheiʔ-naac-ketɔɔʔɔɔ-ninʔɔ."

Nih-ʔii-toun-ɔɔkʔi nohuʔ ʔiθeihyɔhɔʔ. naheiʔiiih
keʔiθinɔɔʔɔɔ-kʔi kɔɔʔɔhwuh. ʔouʔuh-naanʔi.

"ʔiniis-nehtɔnh-aanʔɔ! ʔiniis-nehtɔnh-aanʔɔ! Caaaʔ
nɔnɔɔɔtehi-nɔɔʔ."

ʔouʔuh-kessi-ʔɔɔctaateikouhuʔ nohuʔ kɔɔʔɔhwuh.

Nahaasiiih nohuʔ wɔɔcɔhʔɔɔɔʔ.

Well, once again, now it's the fourth time. Now this coyote set off again from there down the stream. Now, a buffalo bull was lying there, over there. In addition, it was plump. There was a lot of meat on it.

[Coyote] arrived there. This coyote walked all around it. "Hmm, no, it's you, Nih?ɔɔtɔh."

"Well, my turn now. I will show you my power," [said Coyote]. "Here, you must wait for me a while."

After a while, then Nih?ɔɔtɔh set off from there. "I'm going to run off down along the stream." After a while, then Nih?ɔɔtɔh set off from there. Right there, off to the side of the path, in the rocks, he heard a woman. She was crying. A little later he saw her. Then he went over to her.

"Well, what is it, what is it, why are you crying?"

"My father and my mother, they chased me off. I don't have a home. I don't know what I'm going to do. I don't know how I'm going to get by."

"Hmm, I'm here," this Nih?ɔɔtɔh said. "I can take good care of you. We'll be alone together. I can go hunting and so forth. You won't be lacking in anything. You won't be lacking in anything. I will work to provide everything for you We will, it will just be the two of us living together. I will take you home [with me]," this Nih?ɔɔtɔh said.

"Okay," this girl said, "it will be good then, okay."

"Okay, we will move on quickly, but first . . . first, we will kiss each other. We will [kiss], then we'll set off on our way."

Then he took hold of this young girl. Then she changed into a coyote. It was [the coyote].

"I have fooled you! I have fooled you! I am more powerful than you."

Then this coyote ran on off down the stream.

That's how this story ends.

8.

Nih?ɔɔtɔh nɔh ky?ɔɔɔnɔh

Trickster and the Entrails

BY TERRY BROCKIE, BASED ON AN ARAPAHO ORIGINAL, WITH ASSISTANCE FROM ANDREW COWELL

An English-language version of this story is in Curtis 1907-30: 135. In this story, Trickster is once again tricked by Coyote. Perhaps the funniest element of the story is the use of the verb *siiin-* by the coyote when he describes how the fish have taken the entrails from him. This verb means 'raid' or 'plunder' and evokes images of warriors riding into a camp and seizing possessions from others by force. The verb is used specifically for such seizure in the face of resistance (as opposed to sneaking in and stealing something without the owner being aware of it). The contrast between Plains Indian warriors in full battle mode and some fish in a stream supposedly "plundering" coyote gets funnier and funnier the longer one tries to compare the two images. Also very amusing is the fact that the Trickster is so trusting and unsuspicious of the possibility that others might trick him.

(8) Nih?ɔɔtɔh nɔh ky?ɔɔɔ-nɔh

Nih?ɔɔtɔh ?ou?uh-ky?ɔɔɔyaaa?. ?ou?uh-wɔɔtaa-nɔh ky?ɔɔɔ-nɔh; ?ou?uh-nɔɔθoouh kɔɔk?uθaaa?. nah-nii?-k?uθaaa?. Naaneeiyɔɔci-k?uθ-?ɔ ky?ɔɔɔ-nɔh wɔheih byiisiwɔɔ?, ?iikɔn-ɔh, ?aanaasiiih wɔtɔɔsi-nɔh. ?ou?uh-?uu-nɔɔθoouh kɔɔk?uθaa?.

?ɔ?-iisinɔɔ?ɔɔ-ch nohu? kɔɔ?ɔhwuh.

"?ooo?, naaky?aaah! ?ɔɔ-?a-ch?ii-niitehiib-aa??"

"?aaa?, ?ɔɔtɔn-ni?iiih. ?iiyou-nɔh nohu? ky?ɔɔɔ-nɔh. wɔɔw?u ?iniis-k?uθ-ɔwɔɔ?. ?ak-wɔn-eihiiθkii?! ?ak-wɔne-eihiiθkii?. ?ak-k?icaakii?. ?iik?a byɔɔθɔɔciiih ?ɔɔtɔn-biiciwɔɔɔt-ɔwunin?ɔ. ?ɔɔtɔn-touθɔh?ɔwɔɔ-nin?ɔ. ?ɔɔtɔn-biicihi-nin?i."

Nahei?-naac-?atibiθɔkii-k?i kɔɔ?ɔhwuh. ?ou?uh-kebinɔɔ?ɔɔ?. Nahei?-wɔne-eihiiθkii-k?i. Bebiiisiiih ?ou?uh-?eihiiθkii?. nahei?ɔ-ɔtɔɔbe? ?iit?a.

Nahei?-naac-k?in?uθaa-k?i.

Nɔh "?in? nɔwɔhɔ? siniiin-ei?aach. Nɔwɔhɔ? siniiin-ei?aach. Ky?ɔɔɔ-nɔh behi-siiin-ei?aach."

"?aaa? nɔɔθoouh wɔɔtei-ih. ?iiyou-nɔh. Nih-?iis-k?uθ-ɔwɔɔ?. ?ak-wɔne-eihiiθkii?. ?ak-?ɔɔnɔyɔɔhɔw-ɔɔnɔh ?in? nɔwɔhɔ?. nonɔɔɔteh-ch."

?ou?uh-k?i-naac-?atibiθɔkii?. Wɔheih nah-niis-k?ɔ-ɔtɔɔbe?. ?iitaa? ?ou?uh-caac-k?in?uθaa?.

(8) Trickster and the Entrails

Nih?ɔɔtɔh was taking entrails out of game. They were many entrails. He was still cutting them out. That's when he was cutting them out. He was cutting them out cleanly: tripe, well stomach, lungs, various things, intestines, he was still cutting them all out.

Well then this Coyote showed up all of the sudden from out of nowhere.

"Ohhhh, wait! Could I help you?"

"Yes, that will be good. Here they are these entrails. I have already finished cutting them out. Go and wash them! Go and wash them, then bring them back here. Here after a while we will cook them. We will boil them for ourselves so we can eat."

Then coyote took them off over there. There was a stream flowing along there. Then he went to wash them all. He washed them all carefully. Then he gobbled them up over there.

Then he came back here from over there.

And [he said], "Those fish plundered them from me. The fish came on a raid and stole the entrails from me. They cleaned me out."

"Well, there are still plenty of them. Here they are. I have finished cutting them out. Go and wash them. Watch out for those fish. They're tough."

So again [Coyote] took them over there. Well then he ate them up again. From over there he came back here again.

"?iniis-siiin-ei?aach?. nɔnɔɔɔteh-ch? ?in? nɔwɔhɔ?. ?iniis-siiin-ei?aach."

"?aaa? ?iiyou?. nɔɔθoouh wɔɔtei-ih ky?ɔɔɔ-nɔh. nɔɔθoouh wɔɔtei-ih."

Wɔheih nahei-k?i-naac-?atibiθɔkii-k?i. Tɔɔθ?ɔ ?ou?uh-?ɔtɔɔb?i. ?ou?uh-k?in?uθaa?. ?ou?uh-baaan-cɔɔniθaa?.

Nahei?a-aθɔɔhɔb-eik?i. ?ou?uh-?aabitah?aa-?.

"?aaa? wɔɔwɔɔsihiiih, neeih-niiitɔwuun-ɔɔɔk?i.[†] ?ɔh nɔɔθeeih ninaani-n?ɔ ?ohuu-nɔɔ?ɔɔkii-n?ɔ ?iitaa?; nih-?ɔɔ-ɔtɔɔbi-n?ɔ."[‡]

?ou?uh-cɔɔn-kessi-kɔheei? ?ɔɔh ?ou?uh-cɔɔn-nh?ikouhu?.

Nohu? naahaaθɔɔ-h nohu? wɔɔcɔh?ɔɔɔ?. Kibei?iiih ?ou?uh-?ɔtɔɔb?i ky?ɔɔɔ-nɔh nohu? kɔɔ?ɔhwuh. bebiiisiiih ?ou?uh-?uu-wɔne-eihiiθikii-?.

[†]   This is a participle meaning 'the one I asked to do this'.
[‡]   The imperfective prefix *?ii-* has become *?ɔɔ-* prior to the *-ɔ* of the following word.

"They have plundered them from me. They are tough, those fish. They have cleaned me out again."

"Well, here you go. There are still plenty of those entrails. There are still plenty of them."

Well so once again he took them over there. And once again he ate them up. He came back. He could barely walk.

Then [Nih?ɔɔtɔh] noticed that he had a big stomach.

"Hey, you dirty rotten scoundrel, who was asked to do something for me! Maybe it was you who frittered them all away over there. You kept eating them up."

[Coyote] tried but failed to get up and run away. He couldn't run.

And that's how this story goes. This Coyote ate up most of the entrails. He would go and wash them all carefully.

9.

Naakyɔɔɔhʔanʔi ʔikiiθeʔiiwʔɔ

Chief Mountain's Medicine

BY TERRY BROCKIE,
WITH ASSISTANCE FROM ANDREW COWELL

This story tells of the time when the Aaniiih were still residing in Canada. This is the only story in this volume that tells of a vision and the acquisition of sacred power or medicine. Many similar narratives can be found in English in *The Seven Visions of Bull Lodge* (Horse Capture 1980): visions that Bull Lodge shared with his daughter Garter Snake, who then shared them with Fred Gone in the 1930s. Readers may also be interested in *The Gros Ventre Indians of Montana: Volume II* (Cooper 1957), which contains a good deal of information on vision quests and sacred power.

This story is currently known in English. A version of the first part of it is included in Kroeber 1908a: 112-13. Terry Brockie has translated it back into Gros Ventre for this volume, working with Andrew Cowell. Note that Chief Mountain is a place, currently located in the Blackfeet country of northwest Montana, and a well-known landmark. The Aaniiih name for this location is the same as the name of the individual named Chief Mountain in this story. The other personal name in the story, He-Who-Flies-Alone, is a traditional personal name among the Aaniiih. The name belonged to the grandfather of Elmer Main. Elmer was one of the last native speakers of the language, and often worked with Brockie on the language prior to passing away. Since Elmer was born in the 1920s, his grandfather He-Who-Flies-Alone would have been born perhaps in the 1860s or 1870s, if this is the same individual as the one in the story, and the grandfather of He-Who-Flies-Alone would have been born perhaps soon after 1800.

(9) Naakyɔɔɔh?an?i ?ikiiθe?iiw?ɔ

?ɔɔɔyaah, Niisɔh?ohuh ?ibesiiwɔhɔ? ?ohuu-?iiyaa-nic?i,
wɔɔkiiih, ?ɔ?ɔɔɔniiinen-nɔh ?ou?uh-nitɔɔ-nɔh ?in? θaacii?.
Kyaaθey ?ah-niitɔɔtɔsi-ch ?ɔ?ɔɔɔniiinen-nɔh ?ou?uh-wɔn-
nɔkikɔni-nɔh.

Wɔɔkiiih nahei?iiih ?ou?uh-kyessi-biitɔbaa-nɔh.
Byɔɔkouciiih ?ou?uh-?itet-ɔwuuh Ninaasoouh. Wɔɔkiiih
nahei?iiih ?ou?uh-nɔɔhɔɔt-ɔwuuh ?ou?uh-kɔɔ?oouta-n? ?in?
?ɔnɔ?. Wɔɔkiiih nahei?iiih ?ou?uh-nɔɔhɔb-aanɔh ?aabikiiih
?iitaanɔɔn-n?ɔ nou?uθaa-nich ky?ɔtiniih.† Nɔsineeih beh?iiih
?iitaanɔɔn-ninh ?ou?uh-?iyhou?unɔɔ?ɔɔ-ninh ?in? nɔɔtin-?a
?ɔɔkɔciiih ky?ɔtinih.

Wɔɔkiiih ?inen-nɔh ?ou?uh-wɔn-naanyɔhinikii-nɔh. ?ɔɔh
?ou?uh-bii?in-ɔwuuh nɔɔt?a nih-?iit-?iyhou?unɔɔ?ɔɔ-ninh
?iitaanɔɔn-nɔh. Nahei?iiih ?ah-niiθeh-k?i ?inen? ?ou?uh-?ii?:

"Baaniih, kouciiih nɔnoouθaa-nin?i. ?iit?ɔin-inɔɔ? ?ɔɔtɔniiih
?aasiccɔɔ-ch ?aabah-nh?ehi-n?i.‡ ?ɔtooun-nɔk-nɔɔhɔɔcaaa-n?i
?iitaanɔɔn-nɔh ?in? nih-?iit-?iyhou?unɔɔ?ɔɔ-ch."

Nahei?iiih ?itɔɔwucaaa-ch beh?iiih ?inen-nɔh. Wɔɔkiiih
naateiθɔɔɔnaaa-ch nɔh ?ou?uh-?ii?-wɔɔhɔn-touctiki-nɔh
θaanɔɔcii?. Wɔɔkiiih nahei?iiih nɔɔɔt-ɔ? ?i-kɔciyɔn-inɔɔ?
nɔhciiih ?it-eiθɔɔɔn-inɔɔ?, ?ɔɔh ?ou?uh-niiwh?un-ɔwuuh ?i-
kɔciyɔnbiθib-inɔɔ?, toh-biisicaaa-ch ?ohuu-bih?iyɔɔ-h. ?ou?uh-
ciikyaaahkihi-nɔh ?in? nɔɔsin-?a, nɔh ?ou?uh- biisɔɔ?ɔhaaa-nɔh.
?ɔɔtɔɔh ?ou?uh-t?usi-nɔh ?iitaanɔɔn-biihic-ii? ?ou?uh-
?eeinɔɔtaa-ninh biit??ɔwuuh.§

· ·

†   This is a locative form. The base form is *ky?ɔtinih*.
‡   The prefix *?aabah-* requires use of non-affirmative inflections.
§   This is a locative form. The base form is *biit??ɔ́wuh*.

(9) Chief Mountain's Medicine

Long ago, when He-Who-Flies-Alone's grandfather was alive, the Aaniiih were living in Canada. One day seven men decided to go out on a war party.

They left camp on foot. After a while they came to the Sweet Grass Hills. They saw a great deal of dust in the air. Soon they saw big herds of buffalo coming towards the hills. Then all the buffalo disappeared into a hole in the side of one of the hills.

The men went to examine this place. They found the hole where the buffalo had entered. One of them said:

"My friends, we've been gone a long time. Our relatives are going to think that we've been killed. Let's go and examine this place where the buffalo entered."

Everyone agreed. They took off their clothes and tied themselves together with rawhide ropes. They left their guns with their clothes, but they took their ramrods, to feel their way in the dark. They entered the cave quickly, feeling their way along with ramrods. Some of them stumbled over piles of buffalo dung that covered the ground.

Kouciiih ʔeiʔ-iisiθaa-ch ʔinʔ nɔɔtin-ʔa, ʔouʔuh-nɔɔhɔɔt-ɔwuuh ʔɔh-ʔsiisiiyɔɔ-h. Naheiʔiiih touʔuθaa-ch. Wɔɔkiiih ʔouʔuh-chʔeeiʔin-ɔwuuh tɔɔnh ʔaanaasikyɔɔ-nɔɔch. Byɔɔkouciiih ʔeiʔ-iisa-aaniki-ch, ʔɔɔh ʔouʔuh-nʔɔɔbiki-nɔh ʔɔtɔn-nɔnɔɔciiih.

Nɔsineeih ʔouʔuh-nɔɔɔhi-nɔh ʔinʔ ʔɔh-ʔsiisiiyɔɔ-h. Wɔɔkiiih ʔiitʔa ʔɔhwuuuh ʔiitaanɔɔn-byɔɔɔ-nɔh ʔouʔuh-nhʔaanɔɔtaa-nɔh. ʔinʔ ʔinen-nɔh ʔouʔuh-nɔɔhɔɔt-ɔwuuh niicaah, ʔouʔuh-nɔɔhɔb-aanɔh ʔɔhɔɔkinɔh, ʔooh ʔouʔuh-nitouʔ niisiiih niiinɔnʔɔ. Kɔsiiih ʔouʔuh-nɔɔhɔɔt-ɔwuuh ʔaabikiiih ʔɔɔtaa-h, ʔouʔuh-wɔɔtaa-nɔh niiinɔnɔh. Wɔɔkiiih ʔouʔuh-ʔitʔa byiitʔʔɔwuh!

ʔah-niiθeh-kʔi ʔinenʔi ʔouʔuh-thʔii-nʔu-caatɔɔtʔ niisiiih niiinɔnʔɔ, ʔɔɔh ʔinʔ ʔɔɔtɔɔh ʔinen-nɔh ʔouʔuh-tɔnoouhu-ninh, ʔɔh-chʔii-niiwhʔun-ɔwunich ʔi-kɔciyɔn-inɔɔʔ. Wɔɔkiiih naheiʔiiih ʔatib-kʔiθaa-ch ʔinʔ nɔɔsin-ʔa nɔh ʔouʔuh-bhʔi-kʔa-atibkouhu-nɔh ʔinʔ nih-ʔiit-ciikyaaa-ch.

Wɔɔkiiih ʔeiʔ-nɔɔɔhi-nɔh ʔinʔ ʔɔh-ʔsiisiiyɔɔ-h, ʔouʔuh-nɔɔhɔb-aanɔh ʔiisiisiiʔ ʔɔh-khʔu-tɔɔtɔɔniθaa-nicʔi. ʔinʔ ʔiisiisiiʔ ʔouʔuh-nɔɔθɔɔ-naatʔɔɔ-nʔi: ʔouʔuh-chʔii-nhʔɔɔwuθaa-nʔi ʔinʔ ʔɔh-uus-ciikyaaa-nɔh ʔinʔ nɔɔsin-ʔa! ʔinʔ ʔinen-nɔh ʔouʔuh-nɔɔnɔkikɔni-nɔh.

After walking a long way through the cave, they saw light. Then they stopped. They were unsure what to do. After talking for a while, they decided to continue.

Soon they came out into the light. There were many buffalo trails going in all directions. They saw a river, trees, and a single lodge. In another direction, they saw a large camp with many teepees. It was beautiful land.

One man wanted to visit the single teepee, but the others did not want to go, because they did not have their guns. They turned around and went back into the cave. They ran all the way back to the entrance.

When they got back out into the daylight, they saw that the sun was about halfway between rising and noon. It was still in the same place: it had not moved since they went into the cave. They continued on with the war expedition.

Wɔɔkiiih ʔinʔ biikoouh ʔah-niiθeh-kʔi ʔinʔ ʔinen-nɔh, Naakyɔɔɔhʔanʔi ʔi-niishʔiitʔɔ, ʔouʔuh-kɔnaaʔ. Wɔɔkiiih ʔinʔ nih-ʔiis-kɔnaa-kʔi, ʔinʔ nɔɔɔhkeh-kʔi niisiiih niiinɔnʔɔ ʔouʔuh-ʔiteθ-ah. ʔouʔuh-ʔiit-ah:

"Ciniinʔiccɔɔ-nɔɔʔ ʔah-chʔii-nʔu-caatɔɔn-eiʔaaʔ. ʔɔɔh ʔɔɔtɔnɔ-ɔwoounɔn-aanʔɔ nɔh ʔɔɔtɔn-bitaanih-aanʔo. ʔɔɔh ʔɔɔtɔniiih ʔiitɔɔtehi-nʔɔ. Nhʔeh-nahkʔɔ ʔɔɔh thʔii-kyʔɔɔkhʔisin-nahkʔo, ʔiithʔiiihɔʔ wuhnɔtɔɔɔtɔn-eich† ʔateniiyɔɔʔ — ʔooun-nihɔɔyɔɔʔ, nɔh ʔooun-kyakyahiyɔɔʔ wʔataaniiih ʔihkebʔa ʔa-kyʔɔcin-ʔa. ʔaatʔaasib-eich ʔinʔ nihʔɔɔsiih, nɔh ʔiiʔ-kɔteyh-eich ʔouwʔu. Nohuʔ ʔouwʔu, byiitʔɔɔʔ ʔooun-eeibʔ. Naheiʔiiih ciinen-ɔɔnɔɔhaah‡ wɔɔʔtaanehi-nicʔ ʔiicɔɔɔ-nʔ ʔɔt-ɔɔθɔbaah-aʔ, nɔh ʔinʔ ʔiicɔɔɔbisʔi ʔooun-aatʔaataaʔ ʔaniitʔɔɔʔ. Naheiʔiiih ʔiithʔiiihɔʔ yaanʔa niibyaaa-nɔɔhaah.§ ʔiniisi-niibyɔɔɔt-owunɔɔch nohuʔ niibyɔɔɔkʔi, nihii-nɔɔhaah, "Naakyɔɔɔhʔanʔi, wɔɔwʔu ʔooun-tɔwɔcii? nɔh ʔiicɔɔʔ." Tɔtɔh kɔɔkʔusi-nahkʔɔ kyaakyahniiih, nohuʔ ʔi-kiiθeʔiiʔ ʔɔɔtɔn-ʔiiʔ-kʔi-iiyaa-nʔo.

---

† The inflection *-eich* which occurs here and on following verbs is a rare form. It is an indirect imperative. It means 'they must do it to you' but implies more a sense of 'you must make it happen somehow so that they do it to you' (i.e., VTA, 3PL → addressee).

‡ This is an indirect imperative meaning 'you must make it happen somehow so that they do it to that other thing' (i.e., VTA, 3PL → 3.OBV).

§ This is an indirect imperative meaning 'you must make it happen somehow so that they do it' (i.e., VAI, 3PL).

That night one man, whose name was Chief Mountain, had a dream. He dreamed that the owner of the single lodge came to him and said to him:

"It's too bad that you didn't come and visit me. I will take pity on you and give you power. You will be very powerful. If you're killed, and you want to come back to life, you must have your friends paint your body — yellow with black dots from the waist up. They must also point your head to the west, and they must cover you with a buffalo robe. This robe should be one that has the head still attached. They must put a black pipe on your chest, with the pipe stem pointing in the same direction as your head. Then they must sing a certain song four times. After each round of singing, they must say, 'Chief Mountain, it's time for you to get up and smoke!' Even if you are cut to pieces, this power will bring you back to life."

Wɔɔkiiih behiiih ʔɔʔɔɔɔniiinen-nɔh ʔouʔuh-niitɔwɔɔt-ɔwuuh nohuʔ nih-ʔiis-kɔnaa-kʔi. Kyaaθey Naakyɔɔɔhʔanʔi ʔouʔuh-byɔɔɔʔaaʔ, nɔh kyaakyahniiih ʔouʔuh-bisehiʔ ʔiiʔiiih kɔciyɔnɔc-iih nɔh niikyɔhɔʔ. ʔouʔuh-kyʔɔhʔubisehiʔ, nɔh ʔiniithʔiiihɔh ʔouʔuh-ʔiiʔ-iiyouhuu-ninh ʔitɔɔsitʔa ʔinʔ ʔiteniyɔɔɔn-ʔa.

ʔah-niisi-nich ʔiihʔɔhɔh ʔouʔuh-nitɔɔ-ninh nohuʔ nih-ʔiiʔ-byɔɔɔtikiitɔɔn-h. ʔeiʔ-ʔiis- byɔɔɔtikiitɔɔn-h, wɔɔkiiih ʔouʔuh-niisiccɔɔ-ninh ʔɔt-neyaacikii-nich ʔi-kiiθeʔiiwʔɔ. Wɔɔkiiih ʔiihʔɔhɔh kɔɔkɔnɔɔʔɔwuuuh niiskyɔɔ-nich ʔaasiiih ʔeiʔtɔwuuneh-kʔi tih-kɔnaa-kʔi.

Wɔɔkiiih ʔeiʔ-iisiiih niibyaaa-nich, ʔooh Naakyɔɔɔhʔanʔi ʔouʔuh-siikyʔɔɔʔ. Naheiʔiiih wɔkyaanaakii-kʔi ʔiθɔwuuuh ʔɔɔwɔtʔɔɔ-kʔi. Naheiʔiiih wɔɔkiiih tɔwɔcii-kʔi, ʔouʔuh-ʔiten-aaʔ ʔiicɔɔɔ-nʔɔ, naheiʔiiih wɔɔkiiih kyaataakuut-ɔɔkʔi. Nɔh ʔouʔuh-nʔiitehiʔ.

Naakyɔɔɔhʔanʔi ʔouʔuh-ʔiinʔikiiʔ ʔɔnɔɔɔtʔɔ beihʔiiihiiini-kʔi.

All the Aaniiih heard about this dream. One time, Chief Mountain was in a battle, and he was shot with many bullets and arrows. He was killed, and his friends took shelter behind his body.

Two of his sons were there at the battle. After it was over, they decided to try out his power. The sons did just as in the dream.

After the last song, Chief Mountain stretched out. He made a sound like someone who is just waking up. He sat up, took the pipe, and lit it. He regained his full health.

Chief Mountain lived to be an old man.

Niisɔh?ohuh ?ohuu-?ɔnɔh?ihiini-k?i, wɔɔkiiih
Naakyɔɔɔh?an?i ?ou?uh-?atibθoh-eik?i niihiiih niicaahah-a?.
Niisɔh?ohuh ?ou?uh-niitɔwuθaa?. ?in? nih-?iisiθaa-ch ?ou?uh-
?eeinɔci-n?i kiyɔtɔwhɔɔki-n?i. ?ou?uh-kɔnɔh?ehi-n?i, ?ou?uh-
biit?ehi-n?i. Naakyɔɔɔh?an?i ?ei?-iis-ɔɔsii-ciiyei?-k?i nohu?
kiyɔtɔwhɔɔkiin-?a, ?ou?uh-nek?. Wɔɔkiich, tɔh-?ɔɔsii-ciiyei?i-
k?i ?ɔhɔɔkiin-?a, kooun?a ?ou?uh-naa? ?ih-ch?ii-niiskyɔɔk?i.†
Wɔɔkiiih Niisɔh?ohuh ?ou?uh-ch?eei?in-aa?.

Wɔɔkiiih ?ah-niisi-nich Naakyɔɔɔh?an?i ?iih?ɔhɔh
kei?iiih ?ou?uh-th?ii-neyaacikii-ninh ?i-kiiθe?iiw?ɔ, ?ɔɔh ?in?
ninaasɔ?ɔwɔɔ-nic?i ?iih?ɔhɔ? ?ou?uh-ch?ii-th?ii-niiskyɔɔ-
n?i. ?ou?uh-?aasiccɔɔ-n?i Naakyɔɔɔh?an?i ?ɔh-ciineh-k?i.
Naakyɔɔɔh?an?i ?ou?uh-kɔnɔ??aa?, nɔh nih-?ii-cɔɔn-
nɔɔhɔɔcaaa-k?i, nɔh nih-tɔɔtɔθɔyaaa-k?i. Nahei?iiih wɔɔkiiih
ch?ii-neyaacikii-ninh. ?ou?uh-wɔɔtaa-nɔh ?innitaa-nɔh ?ɔ?-?ɔt-
ky?ɔɔkh?isi-? wɔnɔ?.‡

Nahaasiiih.

---

† This is a participle meaning 'his-PAST-not-do that' or 'his thing not to be
done'.
‡ This expression includes the dubitative (doubt) prefix ?ɔ?-, followed by
the future tense. When this prefix is used, iterative inflections are used.
The normal 3S inflection of this verb is -is-?, but the iterative inflection
is -is-i?. The final word wɔnɔ? is used to form the overall expression 'I
wonder if he will come back to life'.

When He-Who-Flies-Alone was a boy, Chief Mountain took him on a walk along a river. He-Who-Flies-Alone was in the lead. On the trail there was a dry, leafless cottonwood log. When Chief Mountain stepped over this log, he died. This was the only thing that he was not allowed to do. He-Who-Flies-Alone had not known about this restriction.

Two of Chief Mountain's sons wanted to try out his power again, but the third son was against it. He thought that Chief Mountain was too old. His face was wrinkled, he could not see well, and most of his teeth had fallen out. For this reason, they did not try out the power. Many people wondered if his power would work again.

That is how the story goes.

Aaniiih/Gros Ventre-English Glossary

This glossary includes all nouns, verbs, particles, and lexical prefixes that occur in the texts in this volume. It does not include inflectional prefixes and suffixes, which are listed separately in the section of the book on language. The order of listing is: a, b, c, č, e, h, i, k, n, o/ɔ (no distinction made) s, t, θ, u, w, y, ʔ. Forms that have a grammatical meaning have that meaning given in all capitals, such as PAST TENSE.

For the prefixes, the final (i/u) should be noted. This (i/u) sometimes appears as /i/ or /u/, but when the following word begins with a vowel, the prefix takes on the value of the following vowel. The prefix may fail to appear at all when the following word begins with a consonant.

When a vowel in the initial syllable of a word does not often appear (typically, when the word has a prefix), the form is given first without the vowel, but then with the underlying vowel, since this sometimes reappears when the form lacks a prefix.

Where a noun is listed with a final hyphen, this indicates that only the full stem of the noun is given, since only that stem occurs in the texts in this volume.

Users of the glossary should be aware that words beginning with ʔ- in Aaniiih often drop this first consonant when there is a preceding prefix. There are no words that actually begin with vowels in Aaniiih, so add an ʔ- to any such form in the texts before you search for it in the glossary.

Also, please look carefully at the discussion of initial change in the language section of the book – without understanding this, you will not be able to find many of the words in the texts.

Abbreviations used here are:

IMPERF	imperfective or habitual aspect
IMPERS	impersonal verb
LOC	locative
NA	noun, animate
NI	noun, inanimate
OBV	obviative
PART	particle
PERS	personal name
PL	plural
PLACE	place name
PREF	prefix
REDUP	reduplicated form
VAI	verb, animate subject, intransitive
VAI.O	indefinite object verb, always ends in *-aaa-*
VAI.T	pseudo-transitive verb, always ends in *-kii-*
VII	verb, inanimate subject, intransitive
VTA	verb, transitive, animate object
VTI	verb, transitive, inanimate object

baaan(i)-   PREF   a little, a little bit; barely
baaanʔo   PART   a little, a little bit; barely
baabenɔɔb-   VTA.REDUP   sniff someone
baacininɔhouhu-   VAI   finish singing (for oneself, about
   oneself?)
baackyɔɔ-   VAI   finish doing something
baačiʔahʔiiih   PART   lots (?) [male form]
baah   NA   friend! (used by men)
baaniih   NA   friends! (used by men)
baas(i)-   PREF   big
baaθeiʔɔɔ-   VII   big, large
baaθih-   VTA   desire someone strongly
bebiiisiiih   PART   properly, thoroughly, carefully
beh(i)-   PREF   all
behiiih   PART   all
behʔiiihiini-   VAI   old man, be a
bihʔih   NA   deer
bihʔiyɔɔ-   VII   dark, nighttime
biicihi-   VAI   eat
biiciwɔɔɔt-   VTI   cook something
biihicʔi   NI   manure, piece of manure
biikiyeeih   NA   chickadee
biikoouh   PART   night, at night
biikʔa   PART   in turn, one after the other; my turn
biisicaaa-   VAI.O   feel, feel things
biisɔɔʔɔhaaa-   VAI.O   feel one's way by means of a tool
biitɔbaa-   VAI   walk, go on foot
biitʔehi-   VAI   bared, naked; leafless
biitʔʔɔwuh   NI   ground, earth
biiwouhu-   VAI   cry
biiʔin-   VTI   find something
bisehi-   VAI   hit, shot, by rock, bullet, arrow, etc.
bitaaa-   VAI   dance
bitaanih-   VTA   give power to someone
bitabyih   NA   old woman
bitɔɔɔh-   VTA   have someone dance, hold a dance for
   someone
bohʔɔɔɔʔ   NA   water monster

byiisiwɔɔʔ NI   stomach of ruminant
byiitɔbaa- VAI   walking, on foot
byiitʔɔɔʔ NI   head
byiiʔinɔɔθibyaa- VAI   find horses
byɔɔkouciiih PART   after a while
byɔɔɔtikiitɔɔni- VII.IMPERS   people are fighting, there is a
   battle
byɔɔɔʔ, full stem byɔɔɔn- NI   road, path, trail
byɔɔɔʔaa- VAI.O   fight, get in a fight or battle
byɔɔɔʔɔɔni- VAI   scout, go on the warpath
byɔɔɔʔɔɔtɔbaa- VAI.O   learn something by scouting
byɔɔθɔɔciiih PART   after a while
bʔ(i)- / biʔ(i)- PREF   just, only
caaayɔʔɔɔtaa- VAI   take someone's virginity
caaaʔ PART   again
caacaabiiih PART.REDUP   off to the side
caac(i)- PREF   to here
caatɔɔn- VTA   visit someone
caatɔɔt- VTI   visit a location, place
caatoouʔɔɔ- VAI   floating this way, this direction
caatɔʔɔɔ- VAI   traveling this way, coming this way
chʔaabah- PREF   don't..., do not...
chʔeeiʔin- VTI   not know something specific
chʔeeiʔinon- VTA   not know someone, not know about
   someone
chʔeeiʔiyaaa- VAI.O   not know, not know things
chʔi- PREF   not, NEGATIVE
chʔiiih PART   not, NEGATIVE
ciicii- PREF   boasting, bragging
ciiciikɔyaaa- VAI.REDUP   swear, curse
ciičeetou- VAI   not present [male form]
ciikyaaa- VAI   enter
ciikyaaahkihi- VAI   run or jump quickly into a place
ciinehi- VAI   old; feeble
ciinen- VTA   put or place something down
ciinib- VTA   quit talking to someone
ciinʔiccɔɔ- VAI   unhappy
ciinʔɔɔ- / ciiniʔɔɔ- VAI   up to no good, do bad things

ciitaʔaanɔɔʔɔɔ- VAI work one's head inside a place
ciitɔɔčeiʔɔɔhu- VAI tied up inside [male form]
ciitɔɔčeiʔɔɔni- VAI tied up inside [male form]
ciiyeiʔi- VAI step, take a step
cɔɔn(i)- PREF unable to....
cɔɔniθaa- VAI unable to walk
cɔɔsʔi, PL cɔɔtɔh NA enemy; Blackfoot
cʔiisikɔh NA duck
cʔɔci- / cɔʔɔci- VAI sit down, sit
čaasɔʔ- VTI close to something, near something [male form]
čaaθaanɔw- VTA think that someone is close by [male form]
čaaθah PART other one, another one, the other one [male form]
čaaθey PART one; once; one time [male form]
čaaθɔɔniiih PART another one [male form]
čaaθɔɔnʔɔ NA.OBV other one, another one, the other one [male form]
česisiiih PART begin, start up [male form]
četɔɔʔɔɔ- VAI set off, depart, get going [male form]
čibiθaa- VAI walk, walk along [male form]
čicikouhu- VAI run away [male form]
činiiθaa- VAI walk a long ways [male form]
čooniiih PART ...ever (whatever, wherever, however, etc.) [male form]
čɔɔɔ- VAI come, arrive [male form]
čɔɔtɔwuuuh PART bravely, courageously, in relation to an enemy [male form]
čɔʔooute- VII high; steep; slope, bank [male form]
čɔʔɔɔʔɔɔ- VII brushy, shrubby [male form]
čɔʔɔtinʔ NI hill [male form]
čyaaʔaanɔɔni- VII there is a noise of something [male form]
čʔiiih / čeʔiiih PART back, returning; again [male form]
kebinɔɔʔɔɔ- VII flowing past (water, for example)
keʔiθinɔɔʔɔɔ- VAI changing, changing into something else
kesisɔhʔuhu- VAI fly away, fly off; start flying
kess(i)- / kesis(i)- PREF start; set off; go away

ketɔɔʔɔɔ-　VAI　set off, depart
kewɔhwɔɔ-　VAI　dance past
kewʔɔɔ-　VAI　get by, survive, make a living
keʔiiih　PART　again; back, returning
khʔ(u)- / kɔhʔ(u)-　PREF　half, halfway
kibeiʔiiih　PART　too many, too much, beyond the limit
kiiθeʔiiʔ,　possessed form kiiθeʔiibʔi　NI　power
kiyɔtɔwhɔɔkʔi　NA　cottonwood tree
kɔciyɔnbiθib-　NI　ramrod, for a gun
kɔciyɔnɔcʔi　NI　bullet
kɔciyʔɔ,　full form kɔciyɔn-　NI　gun, rifle; gun barrel
kɔheei-　VAI　stand up (from sitting)
kɔheeisihkehi-　VAI　jump up, jump to one's feet
kɔhʔɔwuh　NI　coulee, gulch, creek
kɔnaa-　VAI　dream, have a dream
kɔnɔhʔehi-　VAI　dried up, dried out
kɔnɔʔʔaa-　VAI　have a wrinkled face
kɔɔkɔnɔɔʔɔwuuuh　PART　very carefully, meticulously
kɔɔkʔusi-　VAI.REDUP　cut in many places
kɔɔkʔuθ- / kɔɔkɔʔuθ-　VTI.REDUP　cut something out, such as entrails
kɔɔkʔuθaaa- / kɔɔkɔʔuθaaa-　VAI.O.REDUP　cut things out, such as entrails
kɔɔkɔn　PART　for no reason, to no purpose
kɔɔkɔɔnɔɔcɔʔɔɔ-　VAI.REDUP　opening one's eyes
kɔɔnɔɔku-　VAI　open one's eyes
kɔɔθɔh-　VTA　hit or strike someone in the head
kɔɔθɔhaaa-　VAI.O　hit or strike in the head
kɔɔunʔa　PART　only, just
kɔɔʔɔhwuh　NA　coyote
kɔɔʔɔɔuta-　VII　dusty, there is dust in the air
kɔsiiih　PART　elsewhere, in another direction, in another place
kɔsiitiniih　PART　suddenly
kɔsikɔɔutis-　VTA　cut someone loose from something
kɔskeeihi-　VAI　plump, fat
kɔteyh-　VTA　cover someone

kouciiih PART for a long time, after a long time

kout?ɔɔ- / **koutɔ?ɔɔ-** VII after a long time has passed

kyaab(i)- PREF off to the side

kyaakyahniiih PART.REDUP everywhere, all over

kyaataakuut- VTA light (a pipe)

kyaaθey PART one; once; one time

kyakyahiyɔɔ- VII.REDUP spotted, have dots

kyess(i)- PREF begin, start

k?aacikouhu- VAI run back home

ky?ɔcin- NI hip(s), waist

ky?ɔh?- VTA kill with a blow

ky?ɔh?ubisehi- VAI shot dead

ky?ɔɔɔkh?isina- VAI be resurrected, come back to life

ky?ɔɔɔyaaa- VAI.O take out entrails

ky?ɔɔɔ? NI entrails, tripe

ky?ɔtinih NI hill

k?(i)- / **ka?(i)-** PREF back; again

k?in?uθaa- / **ka?inɔ?uθaa-** VAI come back, arrive back

k?iθaa- / **ka?iθaa-** VAI return, go back

k?uθ- / **kɔ?uθ-** VTI cut something out, such as entrails

k?uθaaa- / **kɔ?uθaaa-** VAI.O cut things out, such as entrails

naa- VII be the thing, be the thing that...

naaaneeiyɔɔc(i)- PREF.REDUP.IMPERF cleanly

naac(i)- PREF to there, away from here

naacib- VTA challenge someone verbally

naaciih- VTA approach someone, go over to someone's home

naacθɔt- VTA take someone to one's home

naačikouhu- VAI tired from running; die from running too much [male form]

naaky?aah PART wait!

naakyɔɔɔh?an?i PERS Chief Mountain

naani- VAI be the one, be the one who...

naanihi?(i) PREF intensely, rapidly, hard

naanyohinikii- VAI.T.REDUP check up on something, check something out

naas(i)- PREF remaining behind; left behind

naasɔ?ɔwɔɔ- VAI third, be the third one

naataaʔ PART a distant location
naateiθɔɔɔnaaa- VAI take off one's clothes
naatʔɔɔ- VAI remain behind
naaθʔa PART three; three times
nah- PREF that
nahaa- PREF there, at that place
nahaah PART okay! (used by women)
nahaakouhuuh- VTA ride to that place
nahaas(i)- PREF there, that way
nahaasiiih PART that is how; that is what; leave it as it is
nahaasine- VAI lay there, at that place
nahaasiθaa- VAI that is where someone is walking, going
nahaaskyɔɔ- VAI do that way, this way
nahaatisʔɔn- VTA drive or herd to that place
nahaaθɔɔ- VII that is where it is from; that is how it is; that is how it goes (story)
nahaaʔiiʔ(i)- PREF that is when, then
naheiʔ(i)- PREF then, next
naheiʔiiih PART then, next, so then, so next
naheiʔisa- VII that is as far as it goes, that is how it ends
natiθahaʔ NA my wife
nehtɔnh- VTA fool someone, trick someone
neinɔɔʔ NA my mother
neiʔinɔɔʔɔɔ- VII get stuck tight
neki- VAI die
neyaac(i)- PREF try, try to...
neyaacikii- VAI.T try something out
nhʔ- / nahʔ- VTA kill someone
nhʔaakouhu- VAI run scattering in all directions
nhʔaanɔɔtaa- VII laid out in all directions, scattered out
nhʔaatɔɔʔɔh- VTI shatter something to pieces with a tool
nhʔehi- / nahʔehi- VAI killed
nhʔikouhu- / nihʔikouhu- VAI run
nhʔɔɔwuθaa- VAI move, from standing
nih- PREF PAST TENSE
nihii- VAI say something
nihiit- VTI say something specific
nihɔɔyɔɔ- VII yellow

nih?ikouhuuh- VTA ride fast
nih?inaa- VAI insist on something
nih?ɔɔɔn- VTA chase, pursue someone
nih?ɔɔsiih PART west, to / in the west
nih?ɔɔtɔh NA trickster
nii- PREF ONGOING ASPECT
niibineeih PART.IMPERF secretly
niibyaaa- VAI sing
niibyɔɔɔk?i NI song
niibyɔɔɔn- VTA sing for someone
niibyɔɔɔt- VTI sing something
niicaab- VTA sleep with (sexually)
niicaah NI river, stream
niicii- VAI stand
niicɔɔsi- VAI willow, be a
niihiiih PART along, alongside
niii- VAI camp, set up camp
niiin?ɔ NI lodge, teepee
niiitɔwuun- VTA ask someone for something
niikyɔhɔ? NI arrows
niiniisinei- VAI the two of us, us two, we two
niiniistɔn- VTA.REDUP make or do things for someone;
    work for someone
niish?iit?ɔ NI name
niis(i)- PREF alone
niisi- VAI two, be two in number
niisiccɔɔ- VAI think
niisiiih PART single, lone
niisiθaa- VAI get by, make a living
niiskyɔɔ- VAI do something
niiskyɔɔk?i NI what one does, the thing someone does
niisɔh?- VTA name someone; call someone by a certain
    name
niisɔh?ohuh PERS He-Who-Flies-Alone
niistɔɔ- VAI what someone is doing
niitehiib- VTA help someone
niitɔh PART first
niitɔn- VTA hear someone

niitəniki-   VTA.RECIP   kiss each other
niitəətəsi-   VAI   six, six in number
niitəwəət-   VTI   hear something; hear about something
niitəwuθaa-   VAI   walk first, in front, in the lead
niitəwuuuh   PART   first, first of all
niiθehi-   VAI   one, be; be one in number
niiθenəə?   NA   my father
niiθou?   PART   twenty
niiθə?(u)-   PREF   both
niiw-   VTA   marry someone
niiwh?un-   VTI   take something along, carry something
nii?ihih,   OBV **nii?ihyəhə?**   NA   bird
ninaasouh   PLACE   Sweet Grass Hills, MT ('there are three
    of them')
nistoo-   PREF   carefully
nitəə-   VAI   present, be
nitou-   VII   present, be
niyaaθesikouhu-   VAI   rapidly split apart, separate into two
nəč(i)-   PREF   seek, look for [male form]
nəčiičii-   VAI.T   look for something [male form]
nəčiih-   VTA   look for someone [male form]
nəčikəni-   VAI   go on warpath; go scouting [male form]
nəčikəniibaa-   VAI   lead a war party [male form]
nəčinəhəəcəəə?   NI   spyglass, telescope [male form]
nəh   PART   and
nəh w?eeit?a   PART   or
nəhciiih   PART   with, carrying something with one;
    accompanied by someone
nəhu?   PART   this, this one
noh?učesikouhuucaaa-   VAI.O   signal with a mirror [male
    form]
noh?učesikoutən-   VTA   signal to someone with a mirror
    [male form]
nək(i)-   PREF   look for, seek
nəkikəni-   VAI   scout; go on a war party
nəkəteeih   PART   off to the side, away from the center
nənəəciiih   PART   continue, continue on, go on

nɔnoouθaač?i NI venturing out, travelling around [male form]

nɔnoouθih- VTA drag someone out of the water

nɔɔhɔɔcaaa- VAI.O see, see things

nɔɔhɔɔt- VTI see something

nɔɔhɔw- VTA see someone

nɔɔkɔna- VII morning, be; light, get (in the morning)

nɔɔnɔkikɔni- VAI.REDUP go on war party, scout

nɔɔnɔkohu- VAI.REDUP sleep

nɔɔnɔnehi- VAI die, pass away

nɔɔnɔɔ?aaθɔɔtɔn- VTA.REDUP walk around someone

nɔɔnɔnikiit?ɔ NI death

nɔɔnɔɔɔc(i)- PREF.REDUP a whole lot

nɔɔnɔɔ?ouhu- VAI be lacking in things

nɔɔnɔθɔniθaa- VAI.REDUP get going quickly, move on quickly

nɔɔɔhi- VAI come or go outside

nɔɔɔhis?ɔn- / nɔɔɔhisɔ?ɔn- VTA chase someone out, away

nɔɔɔhkehi- VAI own something, be owner of something

nɔɔɔt- VTA leave someone behind

nɔɔɔt- VTI leave something behind

nɔɔɔtehi- VAI tough, strong, powerful

nɔɔɔθaanɔɔni- VII there is a lot of noise

nɔɔsikyɔhɔ? NA antelope, pronghorn antelope (singular **nɔɔsikyih**)

nɔɔsiini- VII there is a hole there

noot?a, full form **nɔɔtin-** NI cave

nɔɔθeeih PART maybe, perhaps

nɔɔθɔɔ- PREF still, continuing to

nɔɔθoouh PART still, continuing to

nɔɔwunɔɔčineihi? NA Sioux Indian

nɔɔ?aa- PREF around (a location)

nɔɔ?ɔɔh- VTA slaughter, massacre

nɔɔ?ɔɔkii- VAI.T use up, fritter away, exhaust supply of something

nɔsineeih PART soon

nɔtinɔɔh- VTI try to see something

nɔθɔθcɔɔhɔw- VTA look at eagerly, with desire or longing

nɔwɔhɔ? NA fish (singular **nɔwuh**)

nowuh- VTA make a motion as if to do something to someone

noʔoouh PART arriving, coming

noʔoouʔoo- VAI arrive at a place by floating, on water

noʔuuθoʔoo- VAI close one's eyes

nʔ(i)- / niʔ(i)- PREF good, well; able to...

nʔiiih / niʔiiih PART good, well; able to...; okay

nʔiitehi- VAI recover health, get well

nʔikii- VAI.T find a solution, fix a problem, make something right

nʔukouhuuton- / noʔukouhuuton- VTA ride to where someone is at

nʔoobiki- VAI agree with each other

nʔ(u) / noʔ(u)- PREF to here, arriving

nʔuθaa- / noʔuθaa- VAI arrive, walk to a place

siiin- VTA rob, raid, plunder from someone

siikyʔoo- VAI stretch out

siiʔihkehi- VAI jump into the water

taabah PART just now

tebʔaakuut- VTA break someone's neck; break off someone's head

teeinooʔoo- VII going back inside something

teeinowoo- VII go inside something belonging to a person, inside a person's container

teeinowuun- VTA put something inside a place for someone

thuuc(i)- PREF why?

thuutehi- VAI who is someone?

thʔii- PREF want to...

tibyaaʔaanaasa- VII sound of a splash

tih- PREF when, since

toh- PREF so that, in order that, in order to

tokohu- VAI flee, run away

tonisoʔooʔ NA anus

tonooʔoo- VII a hole is forming

tonoouhu- VAI unwilling, reluctant; lazy

tooč?i PART where? [male form]

took?i PART where?

toonh PART ...ever (whoever, whatever, wherever, etc.)

tɔɔs(i)- PREF how?

tɔɔsiiih PART how?

tɔɔsɔh- VTA do what to someone?

tɔɔtɔɔkɔɔtɔɔh PART no meaning, nonsense word

tɔɔtɔnɔɔh PART after all, in the end

tɔɔtɔɔnbyiicihi- VAI eat lunch, eat midday meal

tɔɔtɔɔniinit?ɔ NI right between the horns, in the middle of the head

tɔɔtɔɔniθaa- VAI stand in the middle; be midday (sun)

tɔɔtɔθɔyaaa- VAI.REDUP have missing teeth

tɔɔtounɔɔθibyaa- VAI.REDUP capture horses

tɔɔθ?ɔ PART yet again, once again

toouθibyiih[iih] NA swimmer, bather

toouθibyiitɔɔni- VII.IMPERS people are swimming, bathing

too?uθaa- VAI stop walking, stop

tou?uθaa- VAI stop walking, stop

tɔtɔh PART even though, even if

tɔθɔɔ? NI mortar, used by women for grinding and crushing things

touctiki- VAI tie each other together

toun- VTA hold someone; catch someone

tous(i)- PREF somehow or other

touθɔh?ɔwɔɔ- VAI boil / cook something for oneself until tender

tɔwɔcii- VAI stand up, get up from lying position

tɔyɔɔhɔb- VTA wait for, watch out for someone

tɔyɔɔhɔw- VTA wait for, watch out for someone

t?ɔɔt- VTI hit something

t?ɔw- VTA hit; slap

t?usib- VTA throw someone to the ground

t?usi- VAI stumble or trip over something

t?usit- / tɔ?usit- VTI throw something down to the ground

θaacii? PLACE Canada ('in / at the pines')

θaanɔɔc? NA rope

θei?isine- VAI lay

θɔnoouh PART immediately, right away

θɔɔhɔwuunɔn- VTA notice someone

woheih   PART   well, okay

wokyaanaakii-   VAI.T   make a sound, noise

won(i)-   PREF   go and..., go to do....

wonɔʔ   PART   I wonder

wooch?ɔɔʔ   NI   story, narrative, tale

woočii-   VAI   say [male form]

woočiiih   PART   evidently, apparently, DUBITATIVE; like, resembling [male form]

woočiit-   VTA   say something to someone [male form]

woohon(i)-   PREF   together, united

wookiiih   PART   evidently, apparently, DUBITATIVE; like, resembling

wootaa-   VII   many, there are

wootoh   PART   watch out! Get out of the way!

woowoosihiiih   PART   you son of a bitch!

woowʔu   PART   now

wosihooθʔa   NA   horse

wotaakouhu-   VAI   ride to camp; ride to the center or front of the camp

wotaaθaa-   VAI   go to a camp; go to the center or front of the camp

woteeih   PART   to camp, in camp; to or at the front of the camp

wotɔɔsʔi   NI   intestine

wouʔu-   VAI   have sexual intercourse with someone

woʔtaanehi-   VAI   black

wuhnotɔɔtɔn-   VTA   paint something ceremonially that belongs to someone

wuuuh   PART   wow!

wʔataaniiih   PART   black

yaaniʔowɔɔ-   VII   fourth one, fourth time

yaanʔa   PART   four; four times

yah   PART   hey!, gee!

yɔɔtɔnʔa   PART   five; five times

ʔaaaʔ   PART   yes

ʔaabah-   PERF   might, possibly

ʔaabikiiih   PART   big, large

ʔaabitahʔaa-   VAI   have a big stomach

ʔaacinaahiiih   PART   singing
ʔaacineei-   PREF   very, really; truly
ʔaacineeih   PART   very, really; truly
ʔaači-   VAI   talk, speak, say something [male form]
ʔaačiin-   VTA   talk to someone, speak to someone [male form]
ʔaanaasiiih   PART   various things, and so forth
ʔaanaasikyɔɔ-   VAI.REDUP   what one does, what all one does
ʔaanaʔaaʔ   NA   there s/he is
ʔaaniki-   VAI   talk, speak
ʔaanisibeihi-   VAI.REDUP   hurt, injured when thrown to the ground
ʔaas(i)-   PREF   while, as
ʔaasiccɔɔ-   VAI   think
ʔaasichʔiiih   PART   before, not yet
ʔaasiiih   PART   while, as; what, how
ʔaasiθaa-   VAI   where someone is going
ʔaastaaʔ   PART   no way! No sir!
ʔaatiniiih-   VTA   protect someone, take care of someone
ʔaatoouʔɔɔ-   VAI   place where someone is floating to
ʔaatɔs(i)-   PREF   each time, every time
ʔaatʔaataa-   VII   lying or laid facing a certain direction
ʔaatʔaasib-   VTA   lay someone out facing a certain direction
ʔaayouʔ   NA   what?; what is it?; what is the matter?
ʔabyiitɔɔθibiw-   VTA   steal horses from someone
ʔabyiitɔɔθibyaa-   VAI   steal horses
ʔac(i)-   PREF   must, FUTURE IMPERATIVE
ʔačeeih   PART   FUT.IMPER [male form]
ʔačeeitʔɔ   PART   FUT.IMPER [male form]
ʔačinaa-   VAI   approach, get close to, go near to [male form]
ʔah-   PREF   used with number verbs
ʔakisiiθaaʔ   NA   young woman
ʔanaakyaaʔ   NA   buffalo bull
ʔaniitʔɔɔʔ   NI   your head
ʔasin(i)-   PREF   very
ʔateniiyɔɔɔʔ   NI   your body
ʔatib(i)-   PREF   there, over there

ʔatibiiih   PART   there, over there
ʔatibiθɔkii-   VAI.T   take something there, over there
ʔatibkouhu-   VAI   run to there
ʔatibθoh-   VTA   take someone over there
ʔaθɔɔhɔb-   VTA   watch someone, look at someone
ʔaθɔɔhɔbečiič?   NI   mirror [male form]
ʔayɔʔɔɔ?   PART   well...
ʔeeib-   VII   attached, stuck on to something
ʔeeinɔci-   VAI   sitting or lying at a location
ʔeeinɔɔtaa-   VII   lying at a location
ʔeihi-   VAI   said
ʔeihiiθkii-   VAI.T   wash something
ʔeiθɔɔɔn-   NI   clothes, clothing
ʔei?(i)-   PREF   when, once, after
ʔei?iiih   PART   when, once, after
ʔei?tɔwuunehi-   VAI   told about something
ʔe?in-   VTI   know something; know about something
ʔe?inɔn-   VTA   know about someone; find out about
   someone
ʔibesiiwɔhɔ?   NA   his/her grandfather
ʔickuut-   VTA   grab someone, seize someone
ʔiciniitinaan-   VTA   grab someone by the horns
ʔih-   PREF   if it were so, if it has been so
ʔihkeb?a   PART   above
ʔihči?teit-   VTI   strike something with one's foot [male form]
ʔihčɔ?ɔɔtɔn-   VTA   notice, catch sight of [male form]
ʔihčɔ?ɔɔtɔneihi-   VAI   noticed, caught sight of [male form]
ʔih?ɔɔ?   PART   okay!
ʔii-   VAI   say
ʔii-   PREF   IMPERFECTIVE
ʔiicɔɔ-   VAI   smoke (a pipe)
ʔiicɔɔɔbis?i   NI   pipe stem
ʔiicɔɔɔ?   NA   pipe (for smoking)
ʔiič(i)-   PREF   here, to here [male form]
ʔiič?i   PART   here [male form]
ʔiih?ɔhɔh   NA.PL   his/her sons
ʔiii?   NA   snow
ʔiik?ɔ,   PL ʔiikɔnɔh   NI   lung

ʔiikiiʔ   PART   right there
ʔiikʔa   PART   here
ʔiininiini-   VAI   man, be a
ʔiinɔɔnʔɔ   NA   his/her mother
ʔiinɔɔʔaa-   VAI   hunt
ʔiinɔči-   VAI   sit or be scattered in various directions [male form]
ʔiis(i)-   PREF   already; finished, done
ʔiis(i)-   PREF   what, how
ʔiisibihkihi-   VAI   plop down on the ground, throw oneself down on the ground
ʔiisiθaa-   VAI   walk through a place or area
ʔiisiiih   PART   PERFECTIVE
ʔiisiisʔi,   OBV ʔiisiisiiʔ   NA   sun
ʔiisinaaa-   VAI   finish singing
ʔiisinɔɔʔɔɔ-   VAI   arrive suddenly, show up suddenly
ʔiisiw-   VTA   lay with someone, sleep with someone (sexually)
ʔiiskyɔɔ-   VAI   what someone did
ʔiit-   PREF   where
ʔiit-   VTA   said something to someone
ʔiitaanɔw-   VTA   think that someone is here
ʔiitaanɔɔn(i)-   PREF   buffalo
ʔiitaanɔɔnʔɔ   NA   buffalo; buffalo herd
ʔiitaaʔ   PART   over there
ʔiit(a)hʔiiihɔʔ   NA   your friends
ʔiitɔniiih   PART   on both sides, on both ends
ʔiitɔɔtehi-   VAI   tough, powerful
ʔiitʔa   PART   over there
ʔiitʔɔiʔ,   full stem ʔiitʔɔin-   NA   your relative
ʔiiθaʔaanoou-   VAI   ready, prepared
ʔiiθɔɔhɔɔch-   VTA   show someone something
ʔiiθɔwɔɔʔɔɔ-   VAI   see where one is going
ʔiiwɔɔciisi-   VAI   look secretly, spy(?)
ʔiiwɔɔcɔʔɔɔ-   VAI   peep in, secretly
ʔiiyaa-   VAI   living, alive
ʔiiyouhuu-   VAI   take shelter, hide
ʔiiyouʔ   NI   here it is

ʔii?(i)- PREF INSTRUMENTAL, by means of; why, the reason why

ʔii?(i)- PREF when

ʔii?iiih PART with, by means of, INSTRUMENTAL

ʔinen?i NA man

ʔiniini- VAI have a wife

ʔiniin?ɔ NA his wife

ʔiniith?iiihɔh NA.OBV his/her friend

ʔininitaa? NA person

ʔinɔneitɔn? NA.OBV his/her riding/saddle horse

ʔin? PART that, that one

ʔisiiθah, PL ʔisiiθeeih NI his/her eye

ʔita- VII pretty, nice, beautiful

ʔiten- VTA get, take someone

ʔiteniyɔɔɔn- NI his/her body

ʔitet- VTI reach, get to a place

ʔiteθ- VTA come upon someone, meet someone

ʔitibehi- VTA caught up to, overtaken

ʔitin- VTA take someone; get someone

ʔitis?ɔn- VTA drive off animals; flush out animals

ʔitiθ- VTA come upon someone, meet someone

ʔitiθiči- VAI come upon each other, meet each other [male form]

ʔitɔɔsit?a PART behind

ʔitɔɔwucaaa- VAI agree

ʔitɔɔwuuuh PART truly, really, in fact

ʔiθaa? NA woman

ʔiθeih, OBV ʔiθeihyɔhɔ? NA young woman, girl

ʔiθɔwuuuh PART like, as if

ʔiwɔsiih NA elk

ʔiwɔsiihɔɔchɔ?ɔɔ? NI elk skull

ʔiwɔsiihɔɔθ?a NA horse (archaic form)

ʔiyeeih?a NI his/her lodge

ʔiyeeih?i- VAI have a lodge

ʔiyhouʔunɔɔ?ɔɔ VAI disappear suddenly, quickly

ʔɔci?ɔɔw- VTA ask someone to do something

ʔɔčinɔ?ɔɔ- VAI sneaking up on, creeping up on [male form]

ʔɔh- PREF when, where

ʔɔhɔɔki- VAI cottonwood tree, be a

ʔɔhɔɔkʔi, full stem ʔɔhɔɔkin- NA tree

ʔohuuuh PART when, where

ʔohuu- PREF.IMPERF when, where

ʔɔhwuuuh PART many, lots

ʔɔhʔɔnaakyaan- NA rock

ʔɔkɔɔc(i)- PREF change, switch

ʔɔnɔhʔah NA young man

ʔɔnɔhʔihiini- VAI young man, be a

ʔɔnɔɔɔtʔɔ PART until

ʔɔnɔʔ NI sky

ʔɔɔchɔʔɔɔʔ, full stem ʔɔɔchɔʔɔɔn- NI skull

ʔɔɔciihihɔʔ NA.PL mice (singular ʔoociih)

ʔɔɔctaateiθaa- VAI walk downstream

ʔooh PART and; but

ʔɔɔkɔciiih PART on the side

ʔɔɔkɔɔc(i)- PREF homewards, to one's home

ʔɔɔnɔčinɔʔɔɔ- VAI.REDUP sneak up on, sneak around and spy on [male form]

ʔɔɔnɔɔsibyih- VTA.REDUP give orders to someone, command someone

ʔɔɔnɔɔwuhčihei- VAI.REDUP run down hills, slopes, etc. [male form]

ʔɔɔɔnʔ PART not yet; before

ʔɔɔɔwouʔu- VAI chokecherry bush, be a

ʔɔɔɔyaah PART a long time ago

ʔɔɔsii- PREF over; across

ʔɔɔsiiih PART to one's home

ʔɔɔtaa- VII camp is set up; a lodge is set up; there is a camp

ʔɔɔtɔɔh NA.PL others, other ones

ʔɔɔtɔɔhɔɔʔ NI hammer

ʔɔɔθaa- VAI let's go

ʔɔɔθɔbaah NI chest (part of the body)

ʔɔouckuukii- VAI.T throw something up so that it hangs from something else

ʔɔouta- VII hang

ʔɔɔwouubeihi- VAI feel self going down

ʔouwʔu NI blanket, robe

ʔɔɔwuhčihei- VAI run down (slope, hill, etc.) [male form]
ʔɔɔwuniihiθaa- VAI walk downstream
ʔɔɔwuniihoouʔɔɔ- VAI float downstream
ʔɔɔwunihʔkouhu- VAI run down
ʔɔθaanɔh NI meat
ʔɔt(i)- PREF might, should
ʔɔtɔnah NA your horse
ʔɔtɔn(i)- PREF FUTURE TENSE
ʔɔtɔniiih PART fail, failing
ʔɔtɔniiih PART FUTURE TENSE
ʔɔtɔɔbe- VAI eat up, consume
ʔɔtɔɔnah NA your daughter
ʔɔtɔɔniih- VTA wait for someone
ʔɔtoouhʔ(u)- PREF must, should
ʔɔtooun(i)- PREF must, should
ʔɔθeeihɔɔwuh NI Sun Dance
ʔɔθeeihiinɔhwɔɔ- VAI do a Sun Dance dance
ʔouʔuh- PREF NARRATIVE PAST TENSE
ʔɔwɔɔh PART also, too; even
ʔɔwoounɔn- VTA take pity on someone
ʔɔw(u)huuuh PART many
ʔɔʔ- PREF DUBITATIVE
ʔɔʔeeih PART hey! Gee!
ʔɔʔɔhɔɔh PART ouch! (male speaking)
ʔɔʔɔɔci- PREF facing away
ʔɔʔɔɔɔc(i)- PREF wearing white paint (for scouting or war)
ʔɔʔɔɔɔniinen NA Gros Ventre man
ʔsiisiiyɔɔ- VII sunny, be
ʔuu- PREF same as ʔii-, IMPERFECTIVE
ʔuus(i)- PREF same as ʔiis(i)-